To Greta
Thank you for reading me!
David 2018

The Grateful Disciple
Daring to be Loved

David Wells

contact@davidwellslive.com

D1452413

NOVALIS

Nihil Obstat: Fr Michael Wheaton (Censor Deputatus)
Imprimatur: Bishop Mark O'Toole (Bishop of Plymouth)

Designed by Peena Lad

Published in Canada in 2016 by Novalis

Publishing Office   Head Office
10 Lower Spadina Avenue, Suite 400   4475 Frontenac Street
Toronto, Ontario, Canada   Montréal, Québec, Canada
M5V 2Z2   H2H 2S2

www.novalis.ca

ISBN: 978-2-89688-309-7

Cataloguing in Publication is available from Library and Archives Canada

Published in the United Kingdom by Redemptorist Publications
Alphonsus House, Chawton, Hampshire, GU34 3HQ, UK
Tel. +44 (0)1420 88222, Fax. +44 (0)1420 88805
Email rp@rpbooks.co.uk, www.rpbooks.co.uk
A registered charity limited by guarantee
Registered in England 3261721

Printed in Canada.

We acknowledge the financial support of the Government of Canada through the Canada Book Fund for business development activities.

5   4   3   2   1   20   19   18   17   16

Today too, people prefer to listen to witnesses: they "thirst for authenticity" and "call for evangelizers to speak of a God whom they themselves know and are familiar with, as if they were seeing him."

Pope Francis, *Evangelii Gaudium*

Divine providence is the conspiracy of accidents in our lives through which God speaks, and through which we can detect the movements of grace. Few contemporary spiritual writers read this as astutely as does David Wells. His stories – simple, drawn from ordinary life, yet profound – show us all how God's grace lurks inside our ordinary experience. David Wells reads the movements of grace as a meteorologist reads the weather. This book is a theology of grace.

Ronald Rolheiser OMI
Seminary rector, author and columnist

Looking back we see God trying to reach us through events. The skill is to stay alert and open to him. David tells stories that speak of God not looking on with dismay, but calling upon us to listen to him and to change. This book will encourage you to look at your life through new eyes, so get ready to be surprised by what you discover.

Sr Helen Prejean CSJ
Award-winning author of *Dead Man Walking*

This is an enchanting book; it stands in the ancient Jewish and Christian tradition of talking about God primarily in stories, like Jesus and his parables. The point about stories is that they are open-ended, and invite the reader aboard. David's stories are lively and often very funny, about uncomfortable situations where it turned out that God was waiting for him; and they invite the reader to respond however they will. In addition, each chapter starts with a text from scripture; and you could do worse than simply sit with the text, and ask: why did he choose that one?

Nicholas King SJ
Scripture scholar, author and lecturer

David Wells has given us a spiritual page-turner. Grateful Disciple that he is, he will leave the grateful reader feeling by turns enriched, stimulated, challenged and encouraged by the stories told and the lessons suggested. At this time when Pope Francis calls on every disciple to share their personal encounter with Christ, David shows us how.

Bishop Nicholas Hudson

Jesus knew the power of stories. His parables were rarely about religion, but concerned everyday situations, out of which emerged his teaching and ethics. David Wells is a true evangelist in this way of Jesus. His reflections are moving, powerful, illuminating, Christian and truly Catholic. This book will make you laugh, cry and think about life and faith. Who could ask for more?

Fr Richard Leonard SJ
Author of *Where the Hell is God?*, *Why Bother Praying?*
and *What are We Doing on Earth for Christ's Sake?*

About the author

David is married to Alison. They met in a supermarket when they were young students. She works as an advisory teacher of the deaf and hearing impaired. Their three children, Sam, Matt and Emily, are fast starting adventures of their own.

David was educated at English Martyrs School in Leicester, Keele University, and later in Liverpool, where he trained as a teacher. In 1994 he was awarded a Master of Philosophy degree from Nottingham University. He began his career as a teacher in Ilkeston and went on to work for the Catholic Education Service in London, before becoming an Adult Education Adviser. He worked in the Diocese of Nottingham and then in the Diocese of Plymouth, where he is currently working to support staff in schools. He is a guest lecturer at three universities. This is his second book.

As a public speaker David has had the privilege at leading and teaching all sorts of groups. From speaking to eight thousand young people at Wembley Stadium and similar numbers of teachers in North America, to small groups of men at parish breakfasts or just a few volunteers in a parish meeting.

Also by the same author: **The Reluctant Disciple**

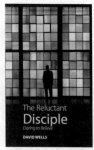

"With self-deprecating humour, David tells gentle stories that describe a powerful Spirit at work in his life."
Fr Christopher Jamison OSB

"... anyone who reads this book can get to know David, be spiritually uplifted, and feel happy being just as God made them."
Most Reverend Malcolm McMahon,
Archbishop of Liverpool

ISBN: 978-2-89688-161-1

For more information see www.novalis.ca

Acknowledgments

With gratitude to the many people who have put their trust in me. Especially but not exclusively, Terry Murphy, Albert Price, Liam Kelly, Mgr Robert Draper, Sr Edith Prendergast, Fr Michael O'Donoghue and Michael Bovill. Their generosity changed the direction of my life, even though I didn't see it at the time. Thanks to all who assisted in the production of this book, and to Caroline Hodgson and Fr Michael Wheaton for their scrutiny.

Dedication

This book is dedicated to the teaching profession, among whom are some of the most remarkable, resourceful and generous people you'll meet. We all know what poor teaching looks like, but the effort and integrity of most staff in schools passes us by, often unseen and unknown.

Contents

Foreword

There are two ways to get a chance to write the foreword in a book. The first, and usual, approach is to become so eminent within a particular field that authors and editors beat a path to your door seeking your recommendation. The second is to wait until a friend of yours writes a book and then to ask him or her nicely. In this case, it was the latter.

I have had the pleasure and blessing of working with David for fifteen years and I am privileged to be able to call him a close friend. I enjoyed the first volume, *The Reluctant Disciple*, immensely and it was understandably well received by very many people.

Now, people being people, it is neither a surprise nor a problem that we have different tastes and I have never known of a work that has truly universal appeal. However, from the conversations I have had about David's book, my concern was that some readers had actually missed what the book had to offer. That some will read it as the author intended and simply find it doesn't "work" for them is probably inevitable. However, as with all writing, if we are misled about what it is trying to do, we will read it from the wrong perspective and ultimately miss the point. So my concern is for those who might otherwise have been richly blessed by the book (or more accurately, by the Spirit working through it) but were prevented from doing so. My response to this is to try to clarify how not to read it and three ways that might bear fruit.

How not to read this book

Each of the chapters opens with an extract from the scriptures. The intention was that this begins to offer a context for the personal anecdotes and reflections that follow. However, this has caused some people to read the rest of the text as though it is an analysis of the scripture itself; what we would call exegesis. If you read the text from that perspective, you are likely to find what David has written quite undeveloped. It is important to understand that these chapters were really never intended to be academic biblical exegesis; you will find your time with *The Grateful Disciple* will bear little fruit if you try to read it from that perspective.

How to read this book

So if it isn't exegesis, what is it? One answer to this is that it is an illustration of an important dimension of the Christian life. That is, we do not believe in a remote God; the God who "lit the blue touch-paper and retired". We believe in a God who is present in the world, who walks alongside us and speaks to us through our life experience – if we have the willingness and capacity to listen. The common theme in David's sharing is what day-to-day life has taught him about himself, about God, about his relationship with God and about his relationship with others. Some people have said to me, "Why do all these things happen to him; my life's nothing like that?" They are wrong. If we have eyes to see and ears to hear, the whole world speaks of God's glory. Sometimes the message slaps us in the face, like Saul on the Damascus road; other times it taps us on the shoulder or whispers in our ear. While this book is about the ways that this has happened specifically to its author, it provides an example and encouragement for us all to reflect likewise on our lives and listen to the Spirit. In sharing his own stories, David illustrates the truth that God is ready to speak to us through the most mundane of our experiences, if we have the wisdom and humility to listen.

In a talk I was giving recently, I referred to *The Reluctant Disciple* as the best book on sin I have read for some time. While the audience were at first taken aback, I stand by it. A Catholic approach to sin has many dimensions but many of us have inherited an undeveloped and often unhealthy (mis) understanding. While we don't express it in these terms, the misunderstanding is about having some form of "bad marks" against our name in some celestial register. While we have been taught this is certain to be the case, we are never quite sure about our current state of reckoning – what "counted" and what didn't – and what we could do to change the marks in the cosmic reckoning book.

This way of thinking, if not taken to the extreme, can perhaps inspire an appropriate humility and a regular inclination to repentance. But even then, this can become rather generalised; a feeling of unworthiness but without any obvious direction of response. A sense of sinfulness that doesn't really help us get anywhere; a spiritual monkey on our shoulder.

An alternative way of understanding is to focus on the notion of *hamartia*. This Greek term, as used by Christian writers for "sin", means to "fall short of the mark", or to "err". Conceived in this way, our sin is not "recorded" in the heavens, but within ourselves. It is not a report card about us but simply the truth of what we have become. It is the extent that we, as we currently are, fall short of God's aspiration for us. Just like when we say a child is "spoilt". We see what the child has become and, even from our earthly perspective, can imagine a better, more developed, more fulfilled version of that child. Happily, as with the child, this is not set in stone. We can know our sin to a great extent and with God's grace can, usually in small steps, make some amends.

So another way to read this book is to see it as David presenting us with his sin. He is rarely the star of his own tales; normally the anti-hero. In each experience he catches himself out and sees the small failings of action or thought that make him a less good father, husband, friend or witness than he would like to be. The beauty and the lesson for us in this is that it is done with positivity and good humour. On each occasion, he experiences some version of the Prodigal's "coming to his senses", and seeing or thinking in a new way. (Which, incidentally, is a more accurate translation of *metanoia* than the usual "repent".) His "sin" is not presented as a millstone, a reason for self-hatred or an unredeemable condition. His capacity for reflection allows the Holy Spirit to hold a mirror up to him and see some new part that needs a little work. While sometimes there might be an element of shame, the overriding response is thankfulness. It is through these lessons that he is helped to emerge a little bit closer to God's aspirations for him than he was before. As C.S. Lewis wrote, "The pains You give me are more precious than any other gains."

For those who might be concerned that I am arguing that we can, by our own efforts, overcome our human concupiscence, please don't worry. Despite chapter after chapter of God's hints at how to be a better David Wells, he's still far from perfect. I know; Alison told me.

On the other hand, it's easy to over-process these things. Perhaps another way to approach this book is just to set aside any preconceptions, read it, enjoy the stories, laugh a little and cry a little and just see what happens. Whichever way you choose to approach this book, I'm glad you've chosen to do so and I highly recommend it, for whatever that's worth.

John Mannix
Chief Executive Officer, Catholic Academy Schools Trust,
Plymouth Diocese

Chapter 1

In a class of my own

If you love me, you will keep my commandments. And I will ask the Father, and he will give you another Advocate, to be with you for ever. This is the Spirit of truth, whom the world cannot receive, because it neither sees him nor knows him. You know him, because he abides with you, and he will be in you. I will not leave you orphaned; I am coming to you. In a little while the world will no longer see me, but you will see me; because I live, you also will live. On that day you will know that I am in my Father, and you in me, and I in you. They who have my commandments and keep them are those who love me; and those who love me will be loved by my Father, and I will love them and reveal myself to them.

John 14:15-21

It all began with a desire to impress. Just twenty-two years old and new in a school, fresh-faced, I wanted to prove to myself and to the teaching staff around me that I could do this job. One day I mused that I too would sit in the staff room talking nonsense as if I wasn't scared out of my mind. So I prepared every lesson with remarkable attention to detail, sitting up until one in the morning trying to find ways to give my teaching both rigour and appeal.

Tuesday afternoon involved an hour in the company of year nine – thirty boys aged thirteen, with more collective testosterone than a battalion of soldiers. This boys' school on Merseyside was not the easiest educational establishment to start a career and this class was one of the school's most challenging. The principal had suggested that I should, "Just sit on them," which I later discovered was a code for "Whatever they do, don't send them to my office." If this was the class everyone feared, I would show the others that I could conquer it. As if climbing onto the back of a wild stallion, I would ride this beast until it surrendered. If I was going to prove my teaching credentials, it would be with this class of Year Nine boys.

On a particular Tuesday morning I had good news. The work they had done at home was, well, done! It wasn't going to win any academic prizes but they had at least worked at home on their projects, every one of them. From a class with such a formidable reputation I had somehow managed to provoke a good reaction. Those more experienced in the art of pedagogy had told me that I would "get nothing out of them," but I had. In the noisy impoverished homes that many of them lived in, they had chosen to get their books out and overcome an overwhelming reluctance to schooling that went back generations. They had done their homework, and we had a reason to be cheerful which I could exploit.

My intention was to join these young people inside their collective sense of persecution and tell them what was possible. "Now you have overcome the first hurdle," I rehearsed; "Now you have shown each other that you are not afraid to work hard, we can begin a real adventure!" I would inspire them to escape their circumstances and rise above a culture of indifference. Those old weary cynics in the corner of the staff room would drop their newspapers and see that these young people were capable of opening their minds.

The classrooms had been built over a hundred years before. The walls were painted glossy white, the contours of bricks and mortar still evident beneath. The windows, high in the walls, ensured that Victorian children would not be distracted by comings and goings outside. Each room was the same size, accessed from long wide corridors, with the same rows of old wooden desks, their inkwells long since unused, and the revolving blackboard behind me. Lights hung from thin metal bars suspended from the high ceiling.

These were the very last days of an era. The photocopier had arrived in the staff room and worksheets were becoming prevalent, but there was still little in the way of technology. Interactive whiteboards and computer-generated images were about to make their entrance. For a hundred years we had written instructions with chalk sticks, but all that was about to change. It was September 1985.

As I arrived to greet the class my hands felt empty. In my haste to be punctual I had left their exercise books in a tidy pile in the staff room. Stupid me. I wanted to show how much their work really mattered and I had managed to forget it – another in a long list of failed good intentions. It was a risk, to leave such high spirits unsupervised, but reluctantly I declared, "I'm out of this classroom for two minutes; if anyone so much as breathes, I'll kill them." As I said it, I pointed in their direction, moving my gaze upon each of them. As I reached the door I added with a practised expression of seriousness, "I'll lose my job, but you'll be dead!" My heartbeat thumping, I ran to the staff room as if my life depended on it.

Down the stairs I run like a hare, skipping most of the steps. Scooping the books in a frantic embrace I return to the classroom with equal urgency. Breathless from the stairs and long corridors, like every teacher I pause outside the slightly ajar door to assess the chaos and how obedient they have been.

Through frosted glass I make out the mayhem. This is not "high spirits" in the way some middle-class schools might describe pranksters, but rather the stomach-churning realisation that there is genuine anarchy. It is like *The Lord of the Flies* in there. The stallion in them has broken out. There is shouting, chasing, wrestling, total chaos. I make out one boy hanging out of the window while one of the others hangs onto his legs. He is trying to wave to the boys in the science laboratory below.

In the few brief seconds which follow I am numb. Almost outside of my own skin, I ask myself, "What am I doing here?" It is moments like this that I become more religious. In my vulnerability, perplexed and confused I pray: "God, I think you want me to be a teacher, but I can't be sure, so help me out here."

My prayer came from the depth of me, and from an uncertainty as to whether I could meet the challenge before me – the challenge posed by these boys. It was not my intention to spend the next twenty years heading for a nervous breakdown only to discover in hindsight that I should never have chosen this career. As a student and an adult I had met people who were never meant to be in the classroom and the worst of them had no idea how bad they were. It was not my wish to join them. So I bargained with God. I wanted God's help one way or another. If I couldn't tame this class, I'd find another career. If I could teach this class I'd need a little divine inspiration. My split-second agony was that I simply didn't know what to do.

Having seen the way they treated their friends I certainly did not want to be one. It was my intuition that I had to go in there hard. Really hard. "I will not show them my fear," I thought. So I inflated myself to my full height, widened my eyes, stressed the veins on my neck and charged the door, all guns blazing. As I kicked the door it hit the front desk with a loud thud. Running in, I positioned myself in front of my desk and bellowed, "Now look!" and after a second's pause, "I trusted you." There was total silence, papers drifted slowly to the floor, fights stopped, faces stunned, eyes fixed towards me.

It was at this moment, the scene before me frozen, that I realised that this was not in fact my classroom. These pupils were not familiar to me. They had no idea who this madman was. This wasn't even my floor. This was the right classroom on the wrong floor. In my anxiety I had run up one flight of stairs too many and each corridor looked exactly the same. In the manner of John Cleese I reversed out of the classroom saying, "Sorry, wrong room!" It was only after the event, when my shock diminished, that I recalled in the corner of my eye, a teacher at the front of the room, looking over his spectacles at this intruder. What on earth did he think he was doing? What did he make of me?

In the corridor I was back with God. "What was that about?" I asked – it wasn't the sort of divine inspiration I had been looking for. Embarrassed and humiliated, I wandered into my classroom with little regard for the prevailing condition of my class. Holding my head in my hands I slumped into the chair at the front of the room, a dejected and failed teacher.

"You won't believe what I have just done," I muttered with the heaviest sigh.

"What did you do, sir?" asked Gary from somewhere near the back.

The question provoked a curiosity from the whole class, as if they were about to be invited into some sort of secret. When I related the events of the previous five minutes the whole class erupted in laughter. As they laughed, they made me laugh. Then it went dramatically quiet. Not the quiet you command or call for. It was the other quiet. The quiet everyone recognises but no one designs. The quiet that takes everyone by surprise. They knew it, I knew it, from the brightest minds to the least able, each of us knew it. For the first time there was a connection between us, and it wasn't in my lesson plan.

Making connections

In asking God to help me out, I got a lesson far more powerful than a different teaching strategy. When I told those young people what had just happened to me in the wrong class we all entered into a new relationship. What they experienced was a teacher who made a mistake and, in a moment of vulnerability, told them about it. I had no idea that telling them about my foolishness would help them to learn to trust me. It wasn't an answer to my prayer that I could have expected.

The grateful disciple has to expect to be taught in unanticipated ways by the presence of God working through us. This is the advocate, the Spirit of God, described in John 14. If I could have given words to what the Spirit was teaching me that day it would have said this: "David, I'm not calling you to teach about me, I am calling you to teach with me." In this scripture we learn that the Spirit is sent to help us. What we are unlikely to know is exactly what that will look like.

I'd been advised not to smile before Easter – to be distant and aloof until my students were subject to my authority. It might have worked for some, but it wasn't working for me. To my surprise they saw something good in my vulnerability, something I couldn't manufacture. Instead of taking advantage of me it was the beginning of a stronger bond. They began to see their teacher not merely as an imparter of knowledge, but a person, a human being. When we influence each other by who we are, we are teaching at a more profound level. We remember our teachers for who they are more than what they taught us.

It wasn't like a Hollywood movie. They didn't change their ways and become reformed citizens. Yet everyone in that class knew there was more to us all than a few lessons and a test at the end of the year. Now there was a potential for the young people to make mistakes too and so risks could be taken, genuine questions could now be asked, and an adventure could begin. It was the silence that taught me this, when for the first time they looked at me and I looked at them, and we both saw something beyond the obvious.

When I came to leave that school, one of the boys said to me, "That crazy thing you did upstairs, Sir, you'll tell that story for the rest of your life." Here was a young prophet, anticipating this very chapter, and how right he was.

Conversation starters

- What are the different levels of "knowing" each other?
- What helps us to trust each other with who we really are?

Chapter 2

The kissing post

From noon on, darkness came over the whole land until three in the afternoon. And about three o'clock Jesus cried with a loud voice, "Eli, Eli, lema sabachthani?" that is, "My God, my God, why have you forsaken me?" When some of the bystanders heard it, they said, "This man is calling for Elijah." At once one of them ran and got a sponge, filled it with sour wine, put it on a stick, and gave it to him to drink. But the others said, "Wait, let us see whether Elijah will come to save him." Then Jesus cried again with a loud voice and breathed his last. At that moment the curtain of the temple was torn in two, from top to bottom. The earth shook, and the rocks were split. The tombs also were opened, and many bodies of the saints who had fallen asleep were raised. After his resurrection they came out of the tombs and entered the holy city and appeared to many. Now when the centurion and those with him, who were keeping watch over Jesus, saw the earthquake and what took place, they were terrified and said, "Truly this man was God's Son!"

Matthew 27:45-54

There is something about officialdom and officials which makes people nervous. The uniform serves to impress upon you that the exchange is not one of equality. Arriving in any country and facing the scrutiny of border controls and security checks leaves us at the mercy of a stranger's judgement. Being humorous or chatty or polite counts for very little in moments like this. The officers are not assessing personality. The question is, are you who you say you are? Are you authentic? There is another dimension to this. I recall pleading in poor French to the manager of a bus depot if I could search his buses for a lost bag which contained five passports. In that moment I was utterly dependent upon his good will. It was very early in the morning and it was within his power to be compassionate towards me, or irritated by me. The rest of our holiday was completely in his hands. In such moments as these we hope for mercy, but we are utterly vulnerable to an official's application of the law.

On the very toe of Lower Manhattan sits a constrained and overshadowed little recreation area known as Battery Park. From there you'll find one of the most poignant views of the United States of America. Across the Hudson River can be seen Lady Liberty, raising her torch to the skies while holding close to her heart the book of the law. She looks towards the ocean and to France, whose gift she was. More importantly, she looks to what was once the most dominant continent in the world, from where she would draw people in their millions. After an often harrowing transatlantic crossing, hers would be the gesture of greeting to a new world and a new life for the immigrants who arrived here. For so many who saw her, there could be no going back. Financial constraint meant a one-way ticket.

We were thrilled to be in Battery Park and looked forward to our visit of one of the world's most famous icons. Our ticket included a visit to the neighbouring Ellis Island Museum. We were aware of this historic immigration port situated in the shadow of the statue, but we had barely paid any attention to it. What took me by surprise was how much more of a lasting impact it made upon me. While no one could deny the visual beauty of the Statue of Liberty, Ellis Island got under my skin and stayed there. In the first half of the twentieth century, twelve million immigrants took their first steps onto this continent at Ellis Island. Today forty per cent of American families have ancestors who landed here. While the iconic importance of the statue is undeniable, to my mind Ellis Island has a much richer lesson to teach us.

On arrival the transatlantic steamships would dock at New York. Health officers would board to check for disease. If the ship passed the test all steerage (third-class) passengers, of which there would often be around three thousand, would be transferred onto smaller ferries to continue on to Ellis Island. First- and second-class passengers went through more up-market immigration at Manhattan.

For all its functional purpose, the immigration hall on Ellis Island is an extravagant building. The Renaissance-style towers and arches are decorated with quoins and carvings. The red brick and limestone layers give it an ornate, almost imposing appearance. Through the doors is a large, chaotic baggage room where immigrants were instructed to leave their worldly belongings. As they arrived they were given an identity tag. Imagine the babies crying, fractious frightened children, weary grandparents and anxious parents, unsure of where to go and what to do. The din in the room was loud, amplified by as many as thirty competing languages.

Immigrants were directed towards the registry which involved ascending a flight of stairs. Unbeknown to them, doctors stood on the balcony beside the stairs, observing any who had trouble walking or breathing. Anyone who displayed signs of ill health was marked with chalk. For example, the letter P indicated pulmonary (lung) problems. X indicated insanity. They then found themselves in the registry, known as the Grand Hall. This huge room was essentially the place to line up for both a medical and a legal examination. These tests marked the essential moments of immigration.

Our entry into the US took us on a similar route, but thankfully without the gaze of a doctor or any chalk mark. When we reached the Grand Hall, I began to sense the fear that the immigrants must have felt when confronted by officialdom. You are vulnerable to a person in a uniform, your life and future are in their hands, and you are just one of thousands. Today that anxiety lingers – a room in which the smell of hope and fear is still tangible.

Doctors conducted a brief "six-second" medical test while people were in line. If they failed, they found themselves detained for further examination at a hospital on the island. Among the tests was a much-feared procedure in which a small tool called a button hook was used to lift the eyelid to test for trachoma, a contagious eye disease. Evidence of the disease often resulted in the person being returned home on the very ship that had brought them. The anxiety was palpable because families could not afford to return together, and at this point they could be separated. If they passed the medical, they proceeded to the legal examination desks.

Seated on tall stools behind high desks at the end of the Grand Hall were the registrars. Each immigrant waited in line to be asked twenty-nine questions which included details about their future plans, their personal finances, where they intended to live and their political views. Those who failed were directed to dormitories where they would await further scrutiny.

Beyond the row of tall desks and uniformed officers was a flight of stairs back down to the ground floor. These steps were divided into three by two rails. Those who were accepted and had plans to head out west and into the interior were guided into the right-hand stairs. Those who were admitted and had plans to head east for New York were directed to the left-hand stairs. Those unfortunate enough to be directed to the middle stairs found themselves in dormitories for further questioning or quarantined in hospital.

At this point, a family knew if it had passed the tests or if their destiny was to be separated. For two hundred and fifty thousand (two per cent) of those who arrived, Ellis Island marked the end of their journey and the start of their return home. It could be devastating. A last and only goodbye. The rails on this staircase represented extremes of elation and relief, or utter distress. These few stairs became known as the "stairs of separation". For joy or sorrow, those who walked them would never forget them.

Reacquainted with their baggage and back on the ground floor, a reception area marked the place where people could greet their loved ones, those who had made it through the arrivals procedure and were joining them in America. It was something akin to the arrivals area in an airport. A pillar in this hall marked a place where people were reunited. To those who worked on Ellis Island, it became known as the "kissing post" – a place of unbridled joy, of tears of relief, marking a new beginning for those who had made it through.

Making connections

On Palm Sunday we listen to an account of the trial, torture and execution of Jesus. In Matthew's Gospel we hear that Jesus cried out before giving up his spirit. At this point the Church kneels in silence. It is a solemn and bleak moment. After the silence, the account becomes apocalyptic, the ground is breaking open, the dead are resurrected from their graves and head for Jerusalem. There in the city there are frequent appearances of the resurrected.

Between the death of Jesus and this turbulence is written one of the most important symbolic moments in Matthew's Gospel. The curtain of the temple was torn in two from top to bottom. Matthew, who is writing with a Jewish audience in mind, is describing something which would have deeply disturbed and shocked his readers. A curtain torn into two can no longer function, it doesn't work as a curtain or shield. Its purpose was to separate the people from the Holy of Holies, the inner sanctuary of the temple. Only the priests could go behind it, while other people were not considered worthy to be in the presence of the heart of God. Only what was deemed pure should come into the presence of purity. Since God is not compatible with impurity, any sin would threaten the presence of God. There was immense fear that if the inner sanctuary became contaminated, God would leave his temple and the people.

Jesus had spent his ministry challenging exclusive religious practices. According to the laws in the book of Leviticus there were many groups who would not be admitted into any part of the temple. These included people with skin diseases such as leprosy, the infirm or crippled, the blind, those who came into contact with the dead, women during menstruation, shepherds, those caught in the act of adultery, foreigners and their servants and convicted criminals. It is no accident that there are specific accounts of all of these groups receiving Jesus' love and acceptance during the course of his ministry.

The final and most inclusive demonstration of God's mercy comes with the removal of the curtain in the temple. In this moment all of creation is invited to see into the heart of God. All that bars or conceals God's love from us is removed. Everyone is invited to reach the kissing post of God, to receive love's embrace, to take our place in the eternal banquet.

This can be too hard for us. We believe that our bad thoughts, our selfishness, our lack of belief, our failures, our corruption and all our many inabilities manage to displease God sufficiently for him to put the curtain back up. Our confidence to approach, to see into God's heart, comes not from our religious accomplishments or social respectability, but from the love of Jesus, whose belief in us makes up for our lack of belief in him.

We have done great damage to ourselves, convincing each other that entry into heaven would be based on our strength and performance. We imagined that the gates to heaven might look like Ellis Island and that purgatory would be like the Great Hall. This denies the role Jesus played in dying for us and opening up for us the heart of God. When you die the encounter will not be with a uniformed official and an X-ray scanner testing for sin and deficiency, rooting out every weakness and deviation. The first encounter will be with the heart of God, the Holy of Holies, whose love for us is overwhelming. I have confidence not in myself, but in the one who made that encounter possible for me.

After death, it may be that the first thing you hear isn't, "Did you pass the test?" but your name, spoken by the voice of love, welcoming you home at last.

Conversation starters

- What image do you have of the gates of heaven?
- Is it helpful or does it give rise to negative thoughts?

Chapter 3

The Christmas tree

I ask not only on behalf of these, but also on behalf
of those who will believe in me through their word,
that they may all be one. As you, Father, are in me
and I am in you, may they also be in us, so that
the world may believe that you have sent me. The
glory that you have given me I have given them, so
that they may be one, as we are one, I in them and
you in me, that they may become completely one,
so that the world may know that you have sent me
and have loved them even as you have loved me.

John 17:20-23

I'm gradually losing it for Christmas. There, amid long aisles of toys piled high into the warehouse ceiling, I watch two young parents trying desperately to placate their screaming children. There is every conceivable toy on display but this is no Aladdin's cave. The children are tired, the toys beyond their reach, the parents look worn out by it all. In their state, I fear they'll forget to purchase the batteries. Christmas has become a season of madness, of frantic purchasing, anxious preparation and profit ratings. It is as if we believe that buying gifts is the only way to communicate love and that drinking is the only way to be merry. At the risk of becoming an old sourpuss, I'm starting to wonder if this is really what makes people happy? Surely there must be better ways to celebrate than by stretching our waistlines and our credit cards to the limit.

The staff at the diocesan office received a call from a parish office asking us if we would provide an Advent study day. Aware of all the parties, shopping and Christmas paraphernalia, the parish council wanted to offer what it called "time out" for people who'd become tired of it all. Since much of the Christmas story stems from Luke's Gospel, we offered a day of reflection looking at the first two chapters and what they might mean for us today. To make it easy for people, we'd provide a crèche, organise a few activities for children, have a good lunch, and try to make it especially welcoming to newcomers. "It would be good", said the priest, "if the day felt like an uplifting gift for stressed-out shoppers."

Arriving early I arranged the chairs in the hall and ran through the arrangements for the day with our small team. To our delight a good number of people began to arrive and we were soon pulling out extra chairs. For a Saturday shortly before Christmas this was a good result. After a big welcome, a short prayer and the children leaving for their activities, the priest left us to attend to his duties and it was time to begin our work together. There was plenty of lively conversation in the room and all looked set for a good day.

Quite quickly it became obvious that the seminar wasn't working. Some faces were looking to the ceiling, others to the floor and some to each other. A man sat forward in his chair, his hands clasped. There was something restless about him and it began to make me nervous. Another lady sat on the second row looking very severe. Nothing was going to make her smile. The usual warm-up jokes I use to help people feel relaxed drew little response. My resourcefulness was drying up quickly. They were not with me. If the day carried on like this it would exhaust us all.

The failure was puzzling me. The material was well researched, the issues pertinent, and there was plenty of room for lively engagement. What was I doing wrong? Nothing quite ages a person like leading a session that isn't connecting with the people it was meant to serve. As I began to wonder what I was doing there so, sadly, was everyone else.

As it was my responsibility to make this work, I stopped what I was doing and said tentatively, "I'm sorry, I think I have started this on the wrong page, do you mind if we have a quick ten-minute break and I'll start again?" They patiently agreed, took another coffee, and got into huddled head-down conversations. Meanwhile I frantically looked through my notes for an alternative approach. Instead of starting with a presentation, perhaps it would be better if we began with some interaction. It might be better to begin by looking at the scripture.

Reconvening the group we began to read together a few of the passages I had taken from Luke's Gospel. The people responded graciously and it provoked some good questions, yet there was still something decidedly uncomfortable about the atmosphere.

During a pause, I finally gave in. "Sorry," I said more assertively. "I'm sorry, but this feels a bit tense to me, does anyone else feel the same?"

The room fell silent. For the first time they were really with me. In the short silence that followed I noticed a small aisle separating the grouped chairs. There was a corridor which hadn't been there when I put them out. This was a room of two groups separated down the middle and by mutual consent. How stupid of me not to see it.

An elderly gentleman eloquently broke the silence: "David, we have always had a Christmas tree on the sanctuary," he said, and pointing a finger in the direction of the gap in the chairs added, "The people from 10am Mass want to move it to the narthex."

A narthex is a porch close to the entrance area of a church. In the early days of the church it was a place for penitents, but these days a narthex acts as an entrance lobby where you will usually find a noticeboard, a collection of dated pamphlets, a pile of hymn books with, "Do not remove from church" written on them and a basket of clothes and smeared cuddly toys left behind from previous occasions. To add further spice to the proceedings the gentleman added, "Father said that we might discuss it today."

Normally it can be hard to work out what the real issues are, but thanks to the gentleman, there it was. An issue named that I couldn't have anticipated. In that moment the good turnout, the gap in the chairs and the distracted group made more sense. They were now looking to me for a resolution. We spent the rest of the morning exploring the origins of the Christmas symbols, their religious roots and whether they really became popular because of Victorian writers such as Charles Dickens. As always, though, the tree did not turn out to be the problem, it was a symptom of the problem.

The Christmas tree had unearthed a divide. There were those who had lived in the parish all their lives. When the Christmas tree arrived on the sanctuary it reminded them of their childhood. It united them with their memories. There was something about that tree that told them that it is still safe and predictable universe. When they saw the tree at the beginning of Advent, it provoked the excitement and anticipation they once knew as children. It was a symbol that the parish belonged to them and they belonged to it.

There was another group which consisted mainly of people who had moved into the parish in the last twenty years. These were less attached to the eccentricities and novelties that emerge during the course of life in a community. The parish priest was well known for leading courses about scripture which had proved very popular. He had encouraged the people to question and challenge each other. To them, the Christmas tree had little to connect it to what happens on the sanctuary or in the liturgy and was much more appropriate for a domestic setting. Perhaps the tree might better be placed in the narthex where it might feature as a seasonal symbol of welcome. On this issue the parish was divided.

There are Christmas-tree issues in most communities. There are those who become attached to how things are, and there are those wanting to ask why things are. When the tension goes unattended it starts to exercise itself over the smaller things, hymn choices, the behaviour of children, or the position of a Christmas tree. The issue itself is normally a symptom of a greater fear. With a little help the divided parish was able to resolve its own problem. They agreed to situate the tree in the narthex and the parish coped generously, but only after they had listened to each other, named their anxiety, and learned how both sides cared about the greater good. Jesus coming into the world brought together kings and shepherds, the most revered and the most despised of men. That is part of what makes for real merriment at Christmas, the healing of the rifts which cause us to put aisles in the chairs.

Making connections

I recall a large sign on scaffolding at Newark Airport apologising for some building work which read, "Excuse our appearance; we are tearing down yesterday to make way for tomorrow." Change can feel like that. Tearing down what has been built and strived for. It can make us protective of our experience and nostalgic for the summers of the past. On the other hand there is a certain decay that comes with resisting change. We become champions of what was, defending it as if it had always been so and blind to new possibility. The tension between progression and conservation is so rarely engaged with and understood that both perspectives back away in fear of what the other represents. It becomes easy to separate and disparage from a distance.

The passage from John's Gospel is often read as a call to the different Christian denominations to become one. This would be one way of reading it, but which overlooks the divisions within our own communities, parishes and extended families. It is remarkable how many of us fall out with each other, preferring avoidance to the long, hard struggle for reconciliation. Here in the passage we are given a tremendous responsibility. The world will not believe in God's love for us if love for each other is not in evidence. It means I have to keep the hand of friendship open, even when it is viewed with suspicion or indifference.

Conversation starters

- What are the Christmas-tree issues in your community?
- What differences in others do we find hard to embrace?

Chapter 4

Love at the school gate

If I speak in the tongues of mortals and of angels, but do not have love, I am a noisy gong or a clanging cymbal. And if I have prophetic powers, and understand all mysteries and all knowledge, and if I have all faith, so as to remove mountains, but do not have love, I am nothing. If I give away all my possessions, and if I hand over my body so that I may boast, but do not have love, I gain nothing. Love is patient; love is kind; love is not envious or boastful or arrogant or rude. It does not insist on its own way; it is not irritable or resentful; it does not rejoice in wrongdoing, but rejoices in the truth. It bears all things, believes all things, hopes all things, endures all things. Love never ends.

1 Corinthians 13:1-8

As young teachers it was not uncommon to have to do what our job descriptions called "bus duty". It entailed standing at the school gate where the buses picked up the students at the end of each day. Getting them safely onto buses was our final duty of care. It was a strange task, unpopular among teachers, who'd normally had enough of separating fights or turning away last year's school-leavers on 50cc mopeds. As an observation in human behaviour, though, it never failed to entertain.

Most striking were the young girls and boys helplessly, almost stupidly, infatuated with each other. Each day these couples had to say goodbye before being apart for about an hour. You'd think one of them was about to emigrate, desperate for a last glimpse before the doors shut and the bus pulled away. What struck me was how public this courting ritual was. You stand in the one place where everyone can see you, and kiss until both lungs have deflated. The rules change with age. When I put my arm around my wife my teenage kids are horrified, but at fifteen you want the world to see that you are lovable.

Love, as far as the school gate is concerned, might be the wrong word. Idolise might be better. She writes his name all over her pencil case. Just take a look at the lyrics they sing in the charts; "You're my world", "You make me complete", "Nothing compares to you". All this reminds me just how complicated and painful being in love at fifteen can be. The liaisons at the gate are moments of needy affirmation. Is the intensity of feeling reciprocated? If it isn't, heartbreak ensues and the lyrics become, "I can't live without you", "I can't go on", "Life has no meaning without you". The bottom falls out of our lives.

The first stage of falling "in love" has been called many things over the years, "flirting" or "making a move". In our part of England, the current terminology is "tapping on". When a boy is "tapping on" to a girl, he's casually flirting or declaring an interest. Recently at a wedding reception I was talking to my daughter when she interrupted and pointed across the room: "Dad, there's a guy over there tapping on to mum." To witness such a challenge when you are fifteen is enough to cause a rush of blood and inflame the male ego. Alternatively, at fifty-one I think to myself, "Oh, this is going to be good!" At fifteen, tapping on is a threat, at fifty-one it is sheer comedy.

After "tapping on" to someone, comes "seeing" them, as in, "I am seeing her." "Seeing" in this context means that they are now a couple, kissing at the gate, but there is strangely no official or formal exclusivity. In some cases it can mean kissing, or in others it might involve sexual relations, but the couple are not committed. The third stage is more formal, which is to declare your status on Facebook. Once you are declared on social media, it's "Hands off! She belongs to me." Being in relationship status on Facebook is a public declaration. It is serious now. All these stages and experiences can be intense, all-consuming and evoke feelings of tremendous jealousy. Falling in love is complicated. Most of us forget the price we paid for discovering that we are lovable.

My father died recently. He was eighty-four. He was surrounded by his family, who were fortunate enough to have sufficient warning in order to be with him in his last few days. We were sitting around him doing our best to support each other. My mother would attend to his every need. As a family we responded to his every utterance, moving him, fetching him a drink, listening attentively to him. There was no time to be wasted. The desire to get things right weighed heavily upon us. We knew this was sacred time. We reminded each other of the stories he told us, about parachuting in the army, or the mischief he got up to as a child. In many of the stories there was immense humour. It is not unusual for joy and sadness to sit closely.

In all the anxiety and stress of these last few days I observed my mum and dad sharing quiet conversation. She was holding tight his hand. They met at a dance when mum was just seventeen. They had no money. Here they were in the late autumn of their lives gazing at each other. I watch how love works now, after sixty years. It is nothing like how it all starts. They both laugh about something. She takes hold of his hand.

"You can go John," she says, adding, "I'll be alright."

He seems to appreciate her permission. They have been looking after each other for sixty years. Letting go is not easy. He breathes a sigh of relief, as if he's had enough of fighting the pain and discomfort of his illness.

"I'll be waiting," he says.

What I observe is that neither is trying to change anything about the other; neither is testing the other's loyalty or seeking affirmation. Neither is in it for themselves. Here is true love, love lived out, challenged by post-war austerity, parenting and ill health. It is not preoccupied by the experience of self, but focused completely on the other. Preparing myself as best I could, I imagined that being together in the last days of my dad's life would be depressing and tragic. Observing love like this had the opposite effect. It gave me a sense of joy and optimism. Our capacity to love and be loved may grow into something far greater than what we first experienced at the school gate.

Making connections

At fifteen we often mistook loving someone for the feeling of affirmation we got from being loved. It can be the feeling of being loved that we fall in love with. After a few years of self-doubt we finally feel special, and so we can idolise the person who makes us feel that way. So it is no surprise that we claim that person entirely for ourselves. We stake our claim and kiss in public places as a mark of ownership. When the feeling wanes we imagine that love has gone and we speak of losing the magic.

St Paul's description of love is not like that at all. In his account, love is less about what we expect from it and more about what we give to it. For St Paul, love generously carries, believes, hopes, endures and ultimately lives eternal. This sort of love is expressed so powerfully in traditional marriage vows: "To have and to hold, for better, for worse, for richer, for poorer, in sickness and in health, until death do us part." These vows speak of living not for ourselves but for the other. They were spoken at the beginning of my parents' marriage but they were never more obvious than in those last days, when they became vivid and real to those of us who were fortunate enough to witness it.

It is a shame that our romantic comedies about falling in love end with a mad dash to the airport, a reconciliation, a plea made on one knee: "Don't go," followed by driving off into the sunset to live "happily" ever after. Happily ever after doesn't come with an instruction manual. It is one thing to have a vocation, quite another to hold onto it. As so many of us discover, it is one thing to get married and another to stay married. It is staying in love that is the greater challenge and if we are fortunate enough to do so, it can help us to become a better version of who we are. We need more love stories from the autumn of life to teach us, not the spring.

Although it can look old and fragile, a love that gives has more to teach us than a love that wants. In the lives of my mum and dad it turned out to be about giving rather than possessing. The last act of true love is to let it go, to permit a goodbye, to forsake being loved and to accept grief. "Happy are those who mourn," Jesus says, but why? Because to grieve means to have loved, and what would a life be without love? We have prized initial attraction as the love story of our age. The truth is the adrenalin rush at the school gate has little to offer that will sustain us. What matters is who we are at the end, not the beginning.

Conversation starters

- What have you learned about love?
- Is love changing you for the better?

Chapter 5

Derek the Atheist

But Thomas (who was called the Twin), one of the twelve, was not with them when Jesus came. So the other disciples told him, "We have seen the Lord." But he said to them, "Unless I see the mark of the nails in his hands, and put my finger in the mark of the nails and my hand in his side, I will not believe." A week later his disciples were again in the house, and Thomas was with them. Although the doors were shut, Jesus came and stood among them and said, "Peace be with you." Then he said to Thomas, "Put your finger here and see my hands. Reach out your hand and put it in my side. Do not doubt but believe." Thomas answered him, "My Lord and my God!" Jesus said to him, "Have you believed because you have seen me? Blessed are those who have not seen and yet have come to believe."

John 20:24-29

Sitting high on a polished wooden stage I am observing all sorts of people arriving in the college hall when I am joined by a fellow panellist. He drags the chair from under the table and swivels it 180 degrees. Sitting down with the seatback in front of him, from his back pocket he pulls a small, folded A4 sheet covered with bold headings and exclamation marks.

"Hi," I say, extending a hand to shake his.

"Hi," he replies.

"All friends now," he smiles, as if anticipating a fight. "Who are you?" he asks.

"I'm David," I reply.

"No, I mean, it sounds a bit like a joke," he says. "Are you the Christian, the Muslim or the Jew?"

"Oh," I say, "Christian – although I'd like to think there was a bit of Hebrew in there somewhere."

He looks at me for a moment expressionless as though assessing his adversary before the fight. Then extending his hand in return he adds, "I'm Derek… the atheist."

Anxious to justify himself he adds, "Science, that's where I put my faith."

As it turns out this antagonist is not from the mosque or the synagogue, but the laboratory.

Approach the West Door of Exeter Cathedral and you are overlooked by dozens of carvings of kings, queens, saints and angels, all set in stone niches. The almost-amusing sculptures are in informal poses, some sitting cross-legged and in apparent conversations with each other. It took over a hundred years to complete this stone facade and it remains as one of the most impressive pieces of medieval masonry in England. Wander through the doors and your gaze is drawn skywards to the ingenious geometry and colourful beauty of the vaulted ceiling. It is impossible to walk around the nave without straining your neck upwards and walking into someone coming the other way. Building work began on this Cathedral in 1133, but most of what we now see was the product of development over a further two hundred years. Apprentices started and finished their careers working on the same building. Exeter is one of several cathedrals like Wells in Somerset and Salisbury in Wiltshire which competed for grandeur and renown in medieval England. These cathedrals are remarkable but for very different reasons.

As you walk up the nave you find yourself beneath and between two square Norman towers, the oldest features of this cathedral. On the inside wall of the North Tower is a wonderful example of medieval science and my favourite novelty in this ornate gothic building – a large astronomical clock.

Before the fourteenth century people measured time largely by a sense of light and darkness with no wristwatches or alarm clocks to organise them. The day was divided into twelve hours between dawn and dusk, with the length of hours stretching in the summer and contracting in the winter. The chime of a bell signalled the call to gather for worship, but this required a way of measuring time. There is some debate as to which medieval cathedral built the world's first mechanical clock, but it is likely that in the early fourteenth century if you knew exactly what the time was, it was because you lived near a cathedral or clock tower.

The astronomical clock in Exeter Cathedral dates back to 1484. On a blue twenty-four-hour dial a golden fleur-de-lys hand indicates the hour, allowing the length of the hours to remain consistent through the seasons. An inner dial with a rotating disc shows the age of the moon and the extent to which it is visible in the night sky. Such was the contrasting pace of life back in medieval times that it was not necessary to add a minute hand for almost three hundred years. A smaller minute dial was added in 1760. Ironically, these days we tend to live by the second and barely notice the years. Beneath the clock is the motto *Pereunt et Imputantur,* "they perish and are reckoned to our account", reminding observers of their mortality and challenging them to value their time. Time was not only to be measured but came with a moral imperative – use it for good, since eventually it will be taken from you!

Beneath the clock is an old seventeenth-century door, notable for the small round hole cut into its base. The incision was made to allow the bishop's cat access to the chamber beneath the clock. It is thought that the animal fat used to lubricate the clock's clunky ironwork attracted vermin, especially mice. The hole in the door may represent the world's oldest catflap. Some people credit this site with the origin of an old nursery rhyme, since hickory was one of the ingredients of the grease:

Hickory, dickory, dock,
The mouse ran up the clock.
The clock struck one,
The mouse ran down,
Hickory, dickory, dock.

While the old door provides us with a lovely myth, the clock is testament to the productivity of the relationship between religion and science. For centuries religious people were leaders in the fields of astronomy, cosmology, calculus and physics. It would have been a complete absurdity to the people who built this clock to ask why anyone would disassociate scientific study and logic from religion and mysticism. Science and religion were seen, not as competitive forces designed to disprove each other, but as complementary and interdependent. Science provoked a greater appreciation for mystery, while religion encouraged curiosity about creation. In the medieval world, an understanding of the sky and the universe would only serve the case for a creator rather than disprove one. To this day, the Vatican has its own observatory, established by Pope Leo XIII in 1891, demonstrating a commitment to science. Amongst its intriguing collections is a world-class selection of meteorites. To place two fields of human enquiry at odds with one another is not an objective fact but an idea.

Close to Exeter lies the stunning Jurassic coastline, a World Heritage Site running from East Devon to West Dorset. It is the only place on earth where the sea has exposed 185 million years' worth of geological history. There inside the cliffs you'll find evidence of ancient red deserts, former coral reefs and sedimentary layers littered with dinosaur bones, limestone twisted and compressed into the blocks which would later be used to build the iconic St Paul's Cathedral in London. Investigate these cliffs more closely and you'll find 185 million years' worth of evidence that God didn't make the world in six days ten thousand years ago, as some creationists assert. Walk on top of the cliffs and you'll stand in awe and wonder before a masterpiece beyond your making. Should you dare to surrender control of it, you'll receive it as a gift, the way creation was meant to be received, with humility and gratitude.

Making connections

Thomas couldn't believe in the resurrection. He couldn't accept the eyewitness accounts of the people he knew as his friends. Thomas wanted evidence. Thomas represents the scientist in us all. He is the one who seeks evidence over testimony. What is intriguing is that Jesus does not condemn Thomas for his doubt or reject him for questioning the accounts of the others. He simply offers an opportunity to conduct the test he requested. This is so vital to a life of faith. Many people misunderstand their own doubts as if they represent hypocrisy or lack of faith. Alongside times of conviction and confidence faith also grows through questioning, testing and moments of disorientation and disbelief. Jesus does not invite his followers to commit intellectual suicide and he did not dismiss their confusion.

When religion loses its desire for reason and ceases to challenge its own practice it becomes fundamentalist and then it indoctrinates. When science loses its capacity for mystery it becomes arrogant and then it exploits the creation it purports to explain. As Pope Benedict XVI said when he visited London in 2010, "The world of secular rationality and the world of religious belief need one another."

The people who built the astronomical clock got it. Standing before a blood-red sunset, a newborn child in an incubator, a vast rolling ocean or at the funeral of a loved one – before the things we question and can't fully comprehend – we can be surprised by a voice of humility within us, one which first asks, "How does that work?" yet can at the same time quietly say, "Thank you."

Back in the school hall that evening my scientist colleague and I had a big problem. Where he saw a contradiction, I saw compatibility. When the influential theologian Blessed John Henry Newman read Charles Darwin's *Origin of Species* at the time of its publication, he reported that there was nothing in it to worry or concern the Church. Similarly, the problem between Derek the Atheist and I wasn't about who would win the battle for the minds of the people, but whether there was a battle to be had at all.

Conversation starters

- Does science pose a challenge to your beliefs?
- What makes you doubt your own beliefs?

Chapter 6

I don't know when it happened

He also said, "The kingdom of God is as if someone would scatter seed on the ground, and would sleep and rise night and day, and the seed would sprout and grow, he does not know how. The earth produces of itself, first the stalk, then the head, then the full grain in the head. But when the grain is ripe, at once he goes in with his sickle, because the harvest has come." He also said, "With what can we compare the kingdom of God, or what parable will we use for it? It is like a mustard seed, which, when sown upon the ground, is the smallest of all the seeds on earth; yet when it is sown it grows up and becomes the greatest of all shrubs, and puts forth large branches, so that the birds of the air can make nests in its shade."

Mark 4:26-32

To this day I don't know when it happened. What I do know is that she walked into my classroom on 3 September 1986. She was tall and striking. There was something about her. She had her hair tied up with ribbons the way Madonna did in *Desperately Seeking Susan*. She wore black gloves with the finger-ends cut off. Despite her beautiful skin she was obviously trying to transgress every make-up rule the school enforced. She didn't need the mascara and the lipstick and she was constantly being sent by senior staff to wash them off. It was quite clear that she wished to make a statement, an impact. She was a girl with attitude. Despite her disguised beauty, Stacey was striking in other ways too. She was angry. Really angry. Angry with the world, angry with her life, angry with authority. She seemed to spend all her time in detention. Some teachers didn't seem to know how to handle her behaviour; one or two were afraid of her.

I don't know when it happened. I do know that Stacey had a way of silencing the entire class. My lessons involved discussions on all sorts of ethical issues, and it wasn't long before Stacey held court. Her forthright confidence was tinged with a brutal and at times savage honesty. She had a way of seeing and naming things without fearing the consequences. It made her both dangerous and powerful. There was something about her that the others either feared or admired. Probably both. After only four weeks with that class no one offered any thought or idea of any consequence. Stacey had a way of exposing other people's weakness and for that reason she could intimidate thirty other students. She could stick the knife into the exact place it would hurt most.

I'm not sure when it happened, but in all the classes I ever taught, she was the only student who ever beat me. Her presence overshadowed mine. Fear of her disapproval eclipsed my attempts at friendly and open classroom discussion. The consequence was a muted class. Occasionally she would catch my eye. I knew she was taking me on. "Who is in charge here?" was the game, and if I made any progress with the others she would see that it would be undone by the next lesson. It was disruption of the cleverest kind because it was passive. It turns out that Stacey wasn't just a pretty face. She was smart too.

I don't know when it happened. It was an annual tradition to take our school-leavers on a "retreat" shortly before they left school. High up in the Peak District they would have a chance to rethink their lives and futures before disappearing from view. It was a good yet tough week for teachers. Spending the week away with the young people was always worthwhile. It was a chance to really meet them properly as people outside of the classroom. The hard side came in dealing with tedious things. Sitting in a corridor on a threadbare carpet until 2am with a cold mug of coffee, ensuring that they stayed in their own rooms, or insisting that they turned their lights out and actually attempted sleep! It was not unusual to get a mere three or four hours sleep a night on these trips.

It was 5am when I got the knock on my door. "Mr Wells, Mr Wells," said a young voice anxiously, accompanied by continued knocking. I leapt out of bed as if I was late for work, disorientated and looking for the light switch, which was in the wrong place because I thought I was at home.

"What is it?" I said, still slapping the wall for that bloody switch.

"We can't find Stacey," came the reply. "We are worried about her."

I quickly came to my senses. There is something terrifying about moments like this. Stacey was in her bedroom when a teacher last checked. Now she wasn't. My stomach flipped. These young people are my responsibility. Whatever private irritations I carried about this girl, I would not wish any harm on her. Jeans over pyjamas, shoes over bare feet, hair like I have had an electric shock, I was quickly in the corridor rallying the other staff to help look for the girl.

It really isn't clear when it happened, but at least for this part of the story the details are precise, because I was fortunate to be the person who found her. For some bizarre reason I looked behind the launderette and down the path that led to a gate and a dry stone wall. There she was, sitting on the wall. It was raining the finest of rain. Without really being aware of it, I was quickly soaked through. Stacey sat nonchalantly, her legs crossed, smoking a cigarette. She didn't acknowledge me. She continued to smoke as if I wasn't there. Sitting next to her on the wall I was experiencing mixed emotions – part relief that she was safe, part anger that she had just put several years on me.

"Stacey," I said, "for two hours until breakfast, you and I are going to pretend we like each other and you are going to tell me what is going on in your head."

A prolonged silence ensued, but I was determined not to fill it. I waited. Eventually, when she cracked, it came out of her like a litany and it went on and on. She told me why she hated her mum, why she hated her stepdad, why she hated her brother, why she hated school, why she hated RE (the subject I taught her), and then she left the best until last. As she pushed the knife in, she twisted it, explaining why she hated me. It was a list I recognised, because the things she named all had a sad element of truth about them. As I sat drenched in drizzle, in the last throws of night-time on that stone wall, listening to my many failings, I wondered if I was being paid enough. What sort of mad job was this? By the time I was at breakfast she had aged me yet again.

I'm not sure when it happened, but ten years later I was sitting at the back of St Barnabas Cathedral in Nottingham. I was at the Sunday evening service which was popular with students and those who hadn't managed to raise themselves out of bed that morning. Mass at the cathedral was an anonymous affair. You could sit in a large sacred space and allow the prayerful atmosphere to wash over you. It was peaceful and undemanding. Womb-like, you could almost hide inside it. My sense of solitude was interrupted by a tap on the shoulder. I glanced behind me to see the girl. Behold the woman.

"I knew it," she whispered excitedly. "I knew it was you. Do you remember me?"

"Remember?" I said. "Are you kidding, Stacey? I have spent the last ten years trying to forget you." We laughed together for the first time.

She was different now. A lot of the make-up had gone. She was still striking, but there was less of a statement going on. Her eyes were not hidden behind dark lines and there was a delight in her smile. As we stood up to leave she took my hand. I was surprised, almost embarrassed. She was always confident, but this was warmth I didn't recognise. There was a new litany. She told me how she'd worked in an office and hated it. Then she took a risk and went to work abroad. The adventure changed her. She worked towards a degree and looked forward to a career in education. She was a different person. She was happy.

Outside now, while walking to her car, she looked up at the cathedral steeple and then looked seriously at me for a moment.

"I come here because of you," she said.

I laughed it off as if it were a joke, but she wanted to impress the point upon me.

"No," she insisted, "you taught me what this means."

Then before getting into her car she kissed me on the cheek and said, "Goodbye Wellsy," which was the name they all called me when they thought I wasn't listening.

I watched that car drive away sensing it would be the last time I ever saw her. It was only as I drove home that night that I realised that I didn't know when it happened. To this day I have no idea what I did for her. The gift was to know I did it. That was enough.

Making connections

Much of society is built upon the idea that we get what we deserve. Work hard and the rewards are there to be enjoyed. We live in a meritocracy. We can begin to believe we have earned all that we enjoy. Jesus challenges this view. It is dangerous to imagine that by our own dedication we get what we deserve because it rules out the opportunity for gratitude. In the scripture there are several parables and teachings which allude to the principle that whatever we have or achieve is God's gift to us. It changes our relationship to everything, even the food we eat or the talents at our disposal.

The seed that grows while no one watches it. "He does not know how", is a beautiful illustration of the teaching. We can plant the seed, we can till the soil, we can reap the harvest, but the growth takes place without us. We cooperate so that God's gift emerges. My student Stacey would grow by God's grace not mine, in her time not mine, in her way not mine. So much so, that while I may have been instrumental in some small way, I have no way of knowing exactly how. I simply don't know when it happened. Most of the good we do is like that. In the end we thank God for it because we know that while we may have been used in some way, the credit isn't really ours. In this way we are saved from our own pride, because God uses us without our knowing how or when.

In 1848, John Henry Newman famously put it like this: "God has created me to do Him some definite service. He has committed some work to me which He has not committed to another. I have my mission. I may never know it in this life, but I shall be told it in the next."

Generally we struggle to think like this. In an outcome-obsessed world we want to predict, measure and reap the rewards of our own dedication. Such an approach to life may appear at first to be motivational, but it denies God's capacity to act inside and behind the scenes of our lives. It takes upon itself the glory. In the end, we take ourselves too seriously and lose our joy when "success" runs out. Once we take control we lose something.

It was a blessed day in 1996 when I met Stacey. Not because she thanked me, but because I was given a rare glimpse of the fruits of my work. The story isn't really about me, it is about all of us. There are many Staceys out there, whose lives are better because of us. It is just that we rarely find out.

Conversation starters

- How do we tend to judge our own worth?
- In what ways might we have a positive impact on others without realising it?

Chapter 7

Imitating the master

Then he poured water into a basin and began to wash the disciples' feet and to wipe them with the towel that was tied around him. He came to Simon Peter, who said to him, "Lord, are you going to wash my feet?" Jesus answered, "You do not know now what I am doing, but later you will understand." Peter said to him, "You will never wash my feet." Jesus answered, "Unless I wash you, you have no share with me." Simon Peter said to him, "Lord, not my feet only but also my hands and my head!" Jesus said to him, "One who has bathed does not need to wash, except for the feet, but is entirely clean. And you are clean, though not all of you." For he knew who was to betray him; for this reason he said, "Not all of you are clean." After he had washed their feet, had put on his robe, and had returned to the table, he said to them, "Do you know what I have done to you? You call me Teacher and Lord – and you are right, for that is what I am. So if I, your Lord and Teacher, have washed your feet, you also ought to wash one another's feet. For I have set you an example, that you also should do as I have done to you."

John 13:5-15

There is little opportunity for privacy once children come along. They burst into life and into your life and, before you know it, even the sanctuary of the toilet is no longer safe from invasion. Hiding there occasionally, it was not uncommon for the door to burst open to the demand of "Dad, will you mend my Buzz Lightyear?" It didn't seem to matter what I was doing, their need came first.

In a world of primary colours, large plastic things to build up or knock down, constantly repeated scenes from a favourite movie and that brief respite after they have gone to bed, life itself was exhausting. We lamented the old days when Sunday mornings included time to read a newspaper and drink strong coffee.

There is also something about having children that makes you self-conscious. Being watched closely chewing, snoring, washing or waking up to a little face three centimetres from your own is challenging. You are being observed, spied upon, and copied almost all of the time, especially when you are least aware of it. Mimicked or impersonated, you'd ask in disbelief, "Do I really sound like that?" There are two such occasions when I found myself being observed very closely.

One morning I became acutely aware of this scrutiny while standing in front of the bathroom mirror. My face covered in shaving foam, I was humming some inane tune from the radio that had woken me up minutes earlier. Bleary-eyed and lacking sleep I sensed I was not alone. Behold the boy, Matthew, knee-height and looking up at me with huge saucer eyes and a runny nose. He pointed to my razor blade, then to the shaving foam. He raised his arms, a means by which he communicated his desire to be picked up. I lifted him onto my hip, my face still covered in foam. With my other hand I drew a smiley face in the condensation on the mirror. He liked it. "Can I do it?" he said. He was drawing on the mirror while I was trying to hold him, shave and pull up my trousers. At the age of four he wanted to be me, poor boy.

Next morning I am ready for him. I find a small mirror to go on the wall at his head height. Taking the blade out of an old plastic razor, I have a handle for him to use. Sure enough, he arrives, trotting into the bathroom. Reaching up, I hand him the plastic razor I have prepared for him. Placing a small amount of foam onto his hand he inspects it carefully and begins to rub it onto his face. We are standing side by side, foam-covered: mine from ear to ear, his pretty much across his face, his head, the wall and now in his eyes. We begin to shave. He is humming some tune as if this is his normal daily routine. We shave together, humming together and then with great big towels we remove the mess from all four corners of the bathroom.

This brief morning ritual became a feature of our daily routine. In he would come, each morning the same. I'd wash my face, he'd wash his. He would wait patiently as I squirted shaving foam into my hand, then I'd squirt some into his. We'd shave off the foam with our razors and wipe our faces. On one occasion I caught him trying to whistle as he shaved. He was learning to be me. Such practices became part of his early childhood. We bought him a plastic lawnmower. When I mowed, he mowed. We bought him a plastic steering wheel. When I drove, he drove. Soon he had a plastic toolkit. When I hit my thumb with a hammer and swore, he hit his thumb and swore.

My other memory of being closely scrutinised was on the banks of the Athabasca River, close to the Canadian town of Jasper, in a small wooded site of pine lodges. We were fortunate enough to be able to stay there for a week one summer when the children were little. There was a site rule about limiting the use of technology. Radios, televisions, personal stereos and phones were tolerated but discouraged. The peace was dominated by the unbroken sound of the wide ice-cold river flowing nearby. It was a wonderful respite from a life generally lived in a state of chaos and unfinished business. Each evening we'd light a fire outside, drink beer and talk to our neighbours. In among all those tall pine trees, deer and elk would roam freely and frequently. In the morning you could open your curtains to find a moose only feet away. It was a great place to bring small children.

Very early one morning, restless and unable to go back to sleep, I got out of bed. The sun was lighting the sky from behind the mountains. Careful not to wake the others I put on a shirt and jeans and went to sit at the trestle table outside our lodge. But for the sound of gushing river water, there was that sort of silence you would only normally get early on Sunday back home. Quite suddenly, a distinctive woodpecker started hammering its beak into a tree close by. The only woodpecker I had ever seen was in cartoons. The sound was exactly as I'd imagined, knocking, almost like gunfire, into the trunk above. Tiptoeing back into the lodge I found a sketch pad and coloured pencils and, anticipating a few hours before the others would emerge, I thought I'd have a go at capturing the scene. With more enthusiasm than talent, I started to draw the bird's legs gripping the bark of the tree.

To my surprise Matthew prised open the lodge door and slipped sideways out. He said nothing, sliding along the bench to join me at the table. The little lad had noticed my absence and, seeing what I was up to outside, searched for the crayons his mum had packed. Sitting at my side he opened up his sketch pad and began to draw the tree in front of him. The two of us sat side by side drawing. It was 6.30am. For some reason I can't explain, I have never felt so important. Sitting together I had to fight off the temptation to tell him he was holding the pencil wrong. It was too precious a moment to make it a teaching opportunity. Something better was happening. I was being paid the ultimate compliment. Love itself was imitating me.

After some time Alison saw what was happening and caught the moment in a photograph. It remains for me one of the happiest memories I possess. A forty-one-year-old and seven-year-old drawing a tree in the woods.

♟Making connections

Two known Sistine Chapel ceilings exist in the world. The first was painted by Michelangelo in the sixteenth century. The second is by Gary Bevans in Goring-by-Sea, West Sussex. During a pilgrimage to Rome in 1987, Gary, a gifted artist and signwriter, noticed that the Sistine Chapel ceiling was almost the same size and shape as his church back home. After gaining the necessary permission from the local priest and diocesan bishop, it took him five and a half years. His replica has received artistic acclaim and has the advantage of being thirty feet lower and therefore nearer to its admirers. Like the original, people have come from all over the world to see it. While gazing upon it, a question comes to mind: is it cheating?

In all my years of schooling and teaching, one of the most consistently disparaged styles of learning was to copy. Copying or imitating was generally assumed to be cheating, and to imitate someone was seen to be lacking honesty and originality. What is striking about the teaching style of Jesus was that it was almost entirely based upon the principle of observation and imitation, an artisan with an apprentice rather than teacher with a pupil. Jesus asked his followers to copy what he did and to learn from the impact it had.

In the passage from John's Gospel the disciples are struggling to understand the point Jesus is making. In response Jesus simply asks them to imitate him. As a master teacher he knows that their understanding will be deeper after the experience. He also knows that the experience of taking part will stay in the memory long after passive knowledge has been consigned to the unconscious. In contrast to most assessments we face in life, regurgitating what is remembered, this is a different kind of test. Jesus encourages his followers to dare to do as he does and then interpret its impact. As Jesus washes the disciples' feet he is no longer instructing them, he is giving himself to them.

In speaking to the Corinthians, Paul drives the point home by both imitating and calling for imitation: "Be imitators of me, as I am of Christ" (1 Corinthians 11:1), he says. John too in his first letter, stresses that believers "ought to walk just as he walked" (1 John 2:6). For the followers of Jesus, copying him was not hypocritical or lacking originality – it was an act of courage which would lead to new and unforeseen possibility.

Most of how we behave comes from imitating things we have seen and value in others. As a parent this becomes an onerous and sometimes frightening responsibility. Everything we do, both good and bad, is observed and practised. How we stand in photos, who we value, what causes us anxiety, how we shave or draw pictures in the woods – everything is watched and practised. These behaviours become part of who we are and then impact on the lives of others. They don't make us cheats or frauds.

When I behave as I imagine Jesus would have, I am not doing it in order to appear as something I am not, but in order to learn from and be changed by the experience. In imitating him I can become slowly, and with a little failure along the way, the very virtue I practise. There are lots of people who will helpfully tell you about virtue. The ones who really make an impact tend to practise them.

Conversation starters

- In what ways is our own behaviour an imitation of others?
- What does it mean to imitate Jesus and what happens when we do?

Chapter 8

Bridging the chasm

There was a rich man who was dressed in purple and fine linen and who feasted sumptuously every day. And at his gate lay a poor man named Lazarus, covered with sores, who longed to satisfy his hunger with what fell from the rich man's table; even the dogs would come and lick his sores. The poor man died and was carried away by the angels to be with Abraham. The rich man also died and was buried. In Hades, where he was being tormented, he looked up and saw Abraham far away with Lazarus by his side. He called out, "Father Abraham, have mercy on me, and send Lazarus to dip the tip of his finger in water and cool my tongue; for I am in agony in these flames." But Abraham said, "Child, remember that during your lifetime you received your good things, and Lazarus in like manner evil things; but now he is comforted here, and you are in agony. Besides all this, between you and us a great chasm has been fixed, so that those who might want to pass from here to you cannot do so, and no one can cross from there to us." He said, "Then, father, I beg you to send him to my father's house – for I have five brothers – that he may warn them, so that they will not also come into this place of torment." Abraham replied, "They have Moses and the prophets; they should listen to them." He said, "No, father Abraham; but if someone goes to them from the dead, they will repent." He said to him, "If they do not listen to Moses and the prophets, neither will they be convinced even if someone rises from the dead."

Luke 16:19-31

Every year over seventy million people pass through Victoria Station in London. Most of them are in too much of a hurry to look around. Some of them wait patiently sitting on their cases or on the floor amongst rucksacks, waiting for a connecting train. In the chaotic terminus you can observe all manner of humanity hurriedly going about its business. It's a colourful, impersonal, tireless, ever-changing scene. It was also the setting for a lesson in my own naïvety and the madness of our world.

With an hour between meetings I found myself in the station concourse perched on one of those tall, padded, circular stools attached to the front of a coffee bar. An hour is too long to do nothing and too short to go anywhere else. In the coffee bar I would catch up on a few calls, grab a sandwich and do a little people watching. It was impossible not to be fascinated. I was like a bird on a wire, observing from a distance.

In front of me a man was gliding a rotating floor polisher back and forth across a gleaming floor. A businessman was remonstrating loudly with someone on his mobile, also pacing back and forth, again and again across the same space. Two middle-aged women pulling cases on wheels greeted each other in shrill voices, before quickly heading off, having somewhere exciting to go. In the middle of all this, a young man arrived and stood quite still. He was looking intently around him, but not as though he was looking or waiting for someone. He seemed strangely out of place. It was apparent that he was perusing the scene, turning around several times as he did so. He was carrying a large brown leather satchel on his waist, the strap ran diagonally across his chest and over his shoulder. His white shirt and black jeans looked casual, but he was smartly dressed, unshaven but his hair well groomed. The young man was here with a purpose.

Then he began. Positioning himself in the centre of the concourse he would pace himself skilfully to the stride of a passer-by. Walking with them at their pace he would strike up a conversation trying as he did so to convince them to take something from his satchel. It was amazing how many people brushed him aside. Some didn't acknowledge him, raising a hand as if to dismiss him, others gave a "No thank you," and some put out a hand as if to accept his offering, but pretty much ignored the conversation. It looked hard – these people were not grateful to have their journey interrupted. Having completed fifty paces with a person he would let them go, turn 180 degrees, and begin the process all over again with someone else. In the short time I watched him, he must have attempted the exercise about twenty times and only two people broke their stride to listen to him. As he came close to me I caught a glimpse of what he was offering; it was a well-known cereal bar with a flyer which read: "A healthier way to get to lunchtime." I admired his perseverance, cheerfully thanking people as they walked away from him.

My attention moved on. On the floor between the coffee bar and a burger outlet was an upright pair of shoes sticking out from under a dirty red tartan blanket. I'd not noticed the feet before, but the rotating polisher was now close by and the shoes had stirred. The cleaner had stopped the polisher and was telling the owner of the shoes to get out of the way. "You know you shouldn't be here," I heard him say. Unlike the shiny floor, the blanket was extremely grimy and so was the man who emerged from under it. He had a ruddy complexion and a short matted beard. His skin was leathery and his eyes glazed. He stood up and was picking up a few things, an empty plastic bottle, a couple of small bags and his blanket. Just as people looked through him and beyond him, he too appeared unaware of his surroundings. They didn't see him, he didn't see them.

The homeless make me uncomfortable. What are you supposed to do at times like this? The professional advice is to support the charities that work with these people, but in the face-to-face moment, it feels callous not to do something about the person you see. At the same time you know that no fleeting gesture is going to resolve the neglect, the mental illness and the addiction that may have brought a man to this state of desperation. As I reflected upon his day ahead, my tall latte, toasted ciabatta with mozzarella and Roma tomatoes (which used to be known as a coffee and cheese and tomato sandwich), seemed a pretentious luxury.

Perhaps this man would be the one person in Victoria Railway Station who would be truly grateful for a healthy cereal bar to get him to lunchtime? I was aware that giving him money would not help him out of his predicament, but perhaps if the man with the satchel could give the man with the blanket a few of those samples, I could buy him a hot drink, and together we'd help him face whatever lay ahead of him that day.

Locating the young man with his food samples, I started pacing up and down the concourse in step with him. He was a student from Milan working temporarily in London. He did not break his pace for me and continued to focus on the commuters. "Please," I asked, "a few bars for the man under the blanket?" He stopped very briefly and glanced for a moment in the direction of the homeless man, who was by now sitting bewildered on one of the station seats. Then he resumed his pace, trying to catch another commuter. As he returned in my direction he stopped to explain, "Look," he said, as if he recognised the predicament, "I can't do that, sorry. We are told not to. It is not what I'm here for." Then he increased his pace for the next passer-by. He returned to his task, and I to my latte. "Of course," I thought, "how stupid of me." It is easy to be generous with someone else's food. I'd seen a simple solution to a complex problem. What I was observing wasn't as easy as a simple redistribution of food. There was something wrong with the situation. So I bought the homeless man a toasted ciabatta with mozzarella and Roma tomatoes.

🔎 Making connections

Many of the stories of Jesus spare us descriptive detail. The tale of the rich man and Lazarus is unusually graphic. It is as if Jesus is trying to drive home a point. Retribution comes through flaming torture to the man who doesn't share his food with poor Lazarus. Most of us would find little difficulty identifying with the moral of the story, if not the imagery, partly because we don't see ourselves as rich. Because we tend to focus on what we don't have, it is so easy for us to lose sight of what we do have. This is more than a story about punishing the greedy.

Earlier in Luke's Gospel, Jesus denounced the Pharisees for focusing on regulation while neglecting the principles of mercy and justice. He chastised them for not heeding the warnings of the prophets. His condemnation was acute because the Pharisees had become caught up in structures which upheld their privilege. It was their collective action which trapped the poor in their condition. After a series of altercations with the Pharisees they rejected Jesus' teaching. In response to their resistance Jesus told the story of Lazarus, about challenging a sinful structure which puts a chasm between itself and the poor and then ignores their cries from the other side.

It is a privilege to live in the United Kingdom. In a table of 142 nations, Britain sits comfortably in the top twenty wealthiest. It is also a country where we give food away to people who might otherwise buy it, and regard it as bad economics to give it to those who might need it most. In Victoria Station some people could have food but didn't want it, while others who needed it were denied it. It was not the young man with the satchel who was at fault, or his employers, but there was something structurally wrong with what was happening. At times, our system rewards the privileged and overlooks the embarrassing poor.

It is my responsibility to ensure that I do what I can for the poor. I also have another responsibility, to challenge the systems which corrupt us, though often unintentionally. We have to be aware that we can all become part of the problem. We can justify our privilege as though it is ours by merit alone, and castigate the poor as undeserving.

An advert next to the burger bar read: "You have the right to what you want, exactly when you want it. Because on the menu of life, you are 'Today's Special'." I wondered what the man under the blanket would make of that?

Conversation starters

- Where do you recognise injustice?
- Are there ways in which our being part of something can make someone else's life harder?

Chapter 9

Untying the tie

Therefore I tell you, do not worry about your life, what you will eat or what you will drink, or about your body, what you will wear. Is not life more than food, and the body more than clothing? Look at the birds of the air; they neither sow nor reap nor gather into barns, and yet your heavenly Father feeds them. Are you not of more value than they? And can any of you by worrying add a single hour to your span of life? And why do you worry about clothing? Consider the lilies of the field, how they grow; they neither toil nor spin, yet I tell you, even Solomon in all his glory was not clothed like one of these. But if God so clothes the grass of the field, which is alive today and tomorrow is thrown into the oven, will he not much more clothe you – you of little faith? Therefore do not worry, saying, "What will we eat?" or "What will we drink?" or "What will we wear?" For it is the Gentiles who strive for all these things; and indeed your heavenly Father knows that you need all these things. But strive first for the kingdom of God and his righteousness, and all these things will be given to you as well. So do not worry about tomorrow, for tomorrow will bring worries of its own. Today's trouble is enough for today.

Matthew 6:25-34

"Don't worry," people say. It seems like useless advice because anxiety is so hard to switch off. I recall my mum ringing me up to ask if I'd bought a coat because the nights were drawing in and winter was approaching. I was in my thirties. "Don't worry," I told her, as if I could deflect the most protective urge with two short words. "I can't help it," she'd say, "I'm still your mum."

It is strange how anxiety works. Anxiety and fear are different. Fear goes away when the threat is removed. Anxiety isn't like that. Anxiety lingers, sometimes nearby but in the background, prodding us when we start to relax. We can put great effort into reassuring ourselves, but then unbidden it returns like an unwelcome guest. Sometimes as I am driving home from work I realise that I am anxious. What troubles me in these moments is not the source of anxiety, but that the cause isn't always obvious to me. At times I have been worried without knowing what I am worried about. Pulling up outside the house I go back through the day, the conversation, the incident that caused the anxiety.

Twenty-five years is a long time to be a school principal. It was my privilege along with colleagues, to attend his leaving Mass and retirement party. He was one of the longest-serving head teachers in our diocese. Such was this man's popularity that the roads around the school were lined with cars squeezed into every available parking space.

Taking seats in the school hall we were surrounded by people who had arrived to express their gratitude. Seats were filled, the walls lined with yet more arrivals. Affections ran deep. Everyone had their anecdote of how this man had turned up on the door when a family was in crisis, how he'd quietly "found the money" to help the most disadvantaged children, how he'd replaced a flat tyre for a despairing parent. There were past pupils of three decades, children, staff, past and present, grandparents, local dignitaries and of course the woman who had stood by his side throughout.

Most moving was the large number of school principals who had come into leadership after him and had sought his advice and guidance over the years. To be appreciated by your peers is a great accolade. One of his fellow headteachers gave a moving speech about how he wouldn't have survived the lonely role without the support of this elder statesman.

"No one quite knows how lonely it is to be the leader of a school," he started, "until you see your name on the sign at the end of the school drive. So I needed help and I would come here to get it. I would ask him to help me tell the difference between a problem that matters and one which doesn't." He emphasised how no one can help as much as someone who has walked the journey ahead of you. No advice rings quite as true as that from someone who has learned through experience.

Here then was a leader who slowly, gently and without intending to draw attention to himself, had worked himself into the affection and appreciation of many generations. When the mayor thanked him for his service to the local community, people stood to applaud, not out of politeness, but out of love. He received the applause reluctantly, wanting desperately to sit down as though he was embarrassed by it all.

Afterwards there was the usual social farewell – quartered sandwiches, chicken on skewers, meandering encounters and opportunists networking. Gradually, people drifted home and the room thinned out until the local parish priest and I found ourselves sitting in the corner with the principal and his wife. He finished this night, as he had so many others, doing the sort of things no one notices, such as throwing a few remaining paper plates into bin bags, checking the windows were locked and the lights off. Then he gave his keys to the priest and invited us back to his home for a nightcap. We left him for a few moments to leave the building for the last time with his wife. They had both dedicated themselves to this place, given more than should ever have been asked of them, and now, whilst deeply relieved that a time for respite lay ahead, you couldn't help but feel that they were saying farewell to something they had loved and suffered for.

At the principal's home we sank into deep sofas and he poured a large scotch into a glass tumbler. Slumping into the chair opposite he proceeded to grasp the knot in his tie and swung it right to left, loosening it and then undoing the top button of his shirt. He expelled a deep sigh. In that moment a dedicated career came to an end.

"The best thing about all this," he said, "is that they can't get me now."

"Sorry?" I said. "Who's out to get you?"

He looked at me with a wry smile. "David," he said, leaning forward, "I have spent my whole life thinking that any day they would walk into the school, discover my paperwork was out of date, that a policy statement was missing or that some deadline had passed me by. They would reveal to the world how close I was to failure."

In the conversation which followed it became clear that while he had no idea what he had done that was so incompetent or negligent, all along he had been quite sure that one day he would be discovered as a fraud. He had lived his life close to the edge of chaos, only just in control.

What made this admission so sad was that despite the overwhelming evidence to the contrary, here was an unassuming and competent leader who had enjoyed little peace of mind. He was the only one who couldn't appreciate his abilities. Despite a lifetime of selfless service, the voice of anxiety had whispered constant threats in the dead of the night. At last the threat was over, he untied the tie for good. I concurred with him – they really couldn't get him now.

Making connections

This beautiful and poetic passage in Matthew's Gospel is encouragement to live by faith. Faith here is understood not in terms of religious conviction, but of what we do with anxiety. Jesus does not want us to live burdened by worry because it debilitates and consumes us and can lead us to seek solace in the wrong places. The passage acknowledges that worry is a feature of our lives: "tomorrow will bring worries of its own."

Experiencing anxiety does not make us faithless, it makes us human. Some people worry more than others, but no life has been lived without anxiety. To avoid it we may chase a few illusory desires, put our trust in flattery, savings, or pension schemes, but these things will not assuage our pain or protect us from our troubles. Look around. The evidence is compelling. People who have more of what they want are no less prone to anxiety.

At first sight, the passage appears like advice from a magazine column: "Worry doesn't help." Jesus isn't telling us not to worry in the way we might say it to each other, hoping to avoid it. Brute strength will only brush our anxieties under the carpet. The school principal accepted that nothing he could do would make them go away, so he learned to live with them. As night followed day, they accompanied him throughout his career. He could only give them up when the threat of being found out had gone.

This is a consoling passage. Jesus unites our will with his, desiring us to live a life free of pointless, unproductive anxiety. A clue as to how to read this passage can be found in 1 Peter 5:7: "Cast all your anxiety on him, because he cares for you." In the scripture Jesus becomes the source of freedom we long for, since we are advised to entrust our worries to him as often as they visit us. In earthly terms this seems like passing the buck, dumping onto someone else. We foolishly see Jesus burdened by the weight of seven billion people's anxieties. This is not how it works. By setting our sights on the kingdom, on Jesus himself, the nonsense and folly of our anxieties is exposed. In the light of truth they become as nothing, slowly evaporating. So often we see the futility of our worry looking back, but Jesus wants us to trust it looking forward.

Gradually, for those who little by little learn to name their worries and leave them before Jesus, their grip wanes. Eventually the truth does set us free. God desires our happiness and longs for us to loosen the necktie earlier in life.

Conversation starters

- What worries seem reluctant to go away?
- What prayer does this prompt?

Chapter 10

Inşallah

When he entered Capernaum, a centurion came to him, appealing to him and saying, "Lord, my servant is lying at home paralysed, in terrible distress." And he said to him, "I will come and cure him." The centurion answered, "Lord, I am not worthy to have you come under my roof; but only speak the word, and my servant will be healed. For I also am a man under authority, with soldiers under me; and I say to one, 'Go', and he goes, and to another, 'Come', and he comes, and to my slave, 'Do this', and the slave does it." When Jesus heard him, he was amazed and said to those who followed him, "Truly I tell you, in no one in Israel have I found such faith. I tell you, many will come from east and west and will eat with Abraham and Isaac and Jacob in the kingdom of heaven, while the heirs of the kingdom will be thrown into the outer darkness, where there will be weeping and gnashing of teeth." And to the centurion Jesus said, "Go; let it be done for you according to your faith." And the servant was healed in that hour.

Matthew 8:5-13

In the searing midday heat, Istanbul is no place to be caught up in a slow-moving queue. We are standing outside the Byzantine masterpiece Aya Sofya one of the "must-see" buildings of this frenetic city. From among the hordes of tourists and street vendors we move out of the unrelenting sunshine through an unimpressive doorway. Passing through walls of mortar several metres thick we move into an insulated, dark, mysterious and beautiful space.

The people gathered there that day brought home to me the anxiety and confusion of our modern age. To understand why, it is important to understand this building. Aya Sofya was built in the sixth century by the Emperor Justinian I as a church dedicated to St Sophia, the Church of Holy Wisdom. For almost a thousand years, Aya Sofya was a centrepiece for the Eastern Orthodox Church.

The lavish decoration is an indication of the importance of this site. The building is capped by an awe-inspiring dome thirty metres in diameter. The interior walls are decorated with impressive golden tiles, intricate mosaics and remarkable icons of Christ, as teacher and infant, Mary the Mother of Jesus, John the Baptist and angels.

Nine hundred years after it was built, the city was captured by the Ottomans, who recognised the worthiness of the building as a place of worship and transformed it into a mosque. The symbols of Christian worship were removed or hidden and many icons were plastered over. During its time as a mosque, the walls were adorned with beautiful calligraphy quoting the Qur'an.

In an Orthodox church, the high altar and the semicircular apse are aligned to the east and the rising of the sun. In a mosque, worshippers face towards the Kaaba in Mecca, which in the Aya Sofya was a difference of 15 degrees. Gathering for prayer here required worshipping Muslims to orientate themselves 15 degrees away from the direction of the walls. To help orientate the worshippers the Islamic features such as the *mihrab*, from where the imam leads prayers, were situated in line with the direction of Mecca, so these features remain slightly at odds with the direction of the building. It is a strange sight, the effect being something similar to a picture hanging skew-whiff on a wall.

After the creation of the Turkish republic in 1923, the country and the building assumed a more secular direction. With a strong emphasis upon education, Aya Sofya morphed into its third incarnation as a state-owned museum. Gradually its primary purpose was perceived to be a place of learning as an exhibition space. In modern times this became a place of the wisdom of enlightenment and history, rather than the worship of God. The icons and mosaics would be uncovered again, but this time for archaeological reasons.

With me in Aya Sofya are a variety of visitors who are connected to the various eras of this building's history. A couple of American tourists are anxiously trying to locate their tour guide who seems to have gone ahead without them; "Over here," shouts one of them, and they rush to be reunited. To my left a Turkish guide is explaining to his group about the fervent campaign to have Aya Sofya returned as a mosque, an issue of such sensitivity, he laments, that it is featured in the forthcoming national elections. Two women walk past me wearing hijabs. I wonder what they make of the tattoos and pierced tummies of some western women. As we move further inside, a young woman stands transfixed, gazing up at an icon of Christ on the gallery wall. She holds her weighty camera lens with both hands but she is not using it. She stands before a craftsman's work, captivated by his meticulousness in restoring a Christian icon from beneath layers of paint. A small school party of German students arrives. They look bored. Two of them share an earpiece from the same iPod.

There is something remarkable about this present-day scene. In contrast with centuries of people who occupied this building at different times and used it for a variety of purposes, these groups of visitors, from all walks of life and all corners of the earth, find themselves using the building at the same time. We are gathered together physically but there is little connection socially or spiritually. Wisdom has brought us together yet we remain apart. This sacred ground is a profound illustration of what has happened to our world in a very short space of time. We move around inside the space yet remain in spaces of our own. We are both aware and at the same time cautious, even afraid of each other.

As the time to leave draws near, I become anxious to look at an icon I've seen in many books. So far I haven't found it on my brief tour of the site. Keen to catch a glimpse before I leave, I ask a member of staff. He is helpful but surly, pointing me in the direction of an upper gallery without making eye contact. He is stationed in a busy doorway and I wonder if he is irritated by the thankless crowds passing by, or whether it is simply a cultural difference in mannerisms.

Pleased to have seen the icon, I walk past the same man on my way out of the building. I thank him for his help and he replies, "Enjoy your day." He speaks these words to the floor as if he repeats them all day long. "Inşallah," I say in reply. Sadly, I have few phrases in Turkish, but one I've learned from trips to other Muslim countries is Inşallah meaning "God willing". Some Irish Catholics use a similar phrase. When I say it, the man's eyes lift to mine. For a few seconds there is contact and it is not without depth. He rewards my feeble effort by giving me the broadest smile which appears to wrinkle his entire face. Inşallah connects us, not as Muslims of course but as people of faith. We are of different religions, races and probably politics, but in that second a shared conviction that our future lies not in our hands but in God's, gives us a bond which traverses the cultural divide. Perhaps, in this age, this is what wisdom demands of us. Not a global summit or an election but a gesture. We give each other an opportunity. I give him a word. He gives me a smile. After that surely a new door can open.

🏋 Making connections

In the story of the healing of the centurion's servant Jesus is transgressing boundaries. The centurion is part of the regime which would ultimately execute Jesus. He is a foreigner, his presence among the people threatens the very purity of Israel and the people's sense of their own worthiness before God. Working for a centurion would be enough to ban a Jew from entry into the temple. Jesus' encounter with this man would have been outrageous enough, but to then reward him with praise, "Truly I tell you, in no one in Israel have I found such faith", would have felt like a betrayal to many who heard of this conversation. For those following Jesus, this meeting would have been hard to stomach.

Time after time in the scriptures Jesus appears to be remarkably undistracted by the political, "isms" and systems of the people. Instead he consistently looks toward their motivations. Jesus sees the love of the centurion for his servant and his willingness to approach a Jew for help. He understands that the centurion too may suffer indignation from his colleagues. In this passage is something of immense beauty. When political systems, G8 summits, or declarations can't resolve problems, healing can surface in the encounter between people. It is often in this more intimate space where Jesus chose to minister and teach us.

In Aya Sofya wisdom herself has brought together Christianity, Islam and the secular. It is a vivid portrayal of the signs of our times. Here you find tourists from cruise ships identified by tour guides' stickers, Muslim women identified by the hijab, archaeologists identified by the badge they are wearing, Christians with no obvious identification, and thousands of tourists identified by their cameras who would have no reason to visit this place other than because it features in their "must-see" guidebooks. Nowhere quite brings together East and West like Istanbul, a city in two continents.

In a similar mixture of conflicting interests and identities, Jesus chose to give us a stark warning: "I tell you, many will come from east and west and will eat with Abraham and Isaac and Jacob in the kingdom of heaven, while the heirs of the kingdom will be thrown into the outer darkness, where there will be weeping and gnashing of teeth." We should be careful who is excluded. What wisdom gathers, we should be careful not to scatter or divide.

In Aya Sofya, diverse and divided, wisdom cannot be revealed from under the tiles, or from the direction the worshippers face, or to whom the building is to be entrusted. If such a virtue is to surface, it begins with personal encounters between us and what we might discover when we dare to meet one another in the same crowded space. Inşallah.

Conversation starters

- How well do we respond to people who are different to us?
- What are your best virtues to offer people you don't know?

Chapter 11

Nice shoes

I am the true vine, and my Father is the vine-grower. He removes every branch in me that bears no fruit. Every branch that bears fruit he prunes to make it bear more fruit. You have already been cleansed by the word that I have spoken to you. Abide in me as I abide in you. Just as the branch cannot bear fruit by itself unless it abides in the vine, neither can you unless you abide in me. I am the vine, you are the branches. Those who abide in me and I in them bear much fruit, because apart from me you can do nothing. Whoever does not abide in me is thrown away like a branch and withers; such branches are gathered, thrown into the fire, and burned. If you abide in me, and my words abide in you, ask for whatever you wish, and it will be done for you. My Father is glorified by this, that you bear much fruit and become my disciples. As the Father has loved me, so I have loved you; abide in my love. If you keep my commandments, you will abide in my love, just as I have kept my Father's commandments and abide in his love. I have said these things to you so that my joy may be in you, and that your joy may be complete.

John 15:1-11

It is said that you can tell all you need to know about a man by his shoes. I hope not. After one of our pupils had committed several serious misdemeanours we decided to call the police to help us impress upon the boy the consequence of his actions.

His parents feared that if he continued in the direction he was taking he would find himself in the magistrate's court. The policeman gave the boy quite a stern telling off. Then he surprised us by going off script and challenging the boy's appearance, suggesting that he should start to take a greater pride in himself. "Look at my shoes," he said. "Spotless. I brush them every day." Then to endorse his point he said, "And look at Mr Wells' shoes..." Sadly, he had not done his research. Somewhat sheepishly he continued, "Actually, don't look at Mr Wells' shoes."

My dad, who polished his shoes every time he wore them, would have been ashamed of the scuff marks and broken laces which now betrayed my sad lack of self-discipline. I should have known better. A few years before, it was the state of a pair of shoes which led to one of the most vivid examples of Christian love I have witnessed.

Way back in the early eighties a new priest arrived in our parish. He was a curate and this was his first assignment. He was different to many of the other priests I had known. He was younger, loved to talk about sport, enjoyed a pint and drove an Austin Allegro. It was hardly a Porsche, but it became part of his popular appeal. He was good fun. So when he offered to drive four of us across France to the Pyrenean mountains it was an easy decision. As we drove across the vineyards of central France we would stop to sample the local wine in little tents set up by the roadside. It was a beautifully hot sunny day, and while seven hundred million people sat glued to their TV sets watching Prince Charles marry Lady Diana Spencer, I was heading across Charente to stay overnight in Angoulême, where my education in French wine and strong smelly cheese began.

Our destination was a hospital in Lourdes. We were to be working in the hospital from first thing in the morning until early evening. Our duties would include washing, dressing and feeding patients, and then taking them in wheelchairs known as "voitures" to the various religious processions and services – and then to the cafés for beer.

As a young, fit seventeen-year-old, I felt invincible. I would live forever, the solution to my problems was in my own control. My life and my concerns were all about me. Here in Lourdes I was in the presence of those for whom none of that was true. They were vulnerable, some of them dying, some unable to clean their own teeth, yet they were often concerned about each other and their helpers. I was helping to lift a man out of a bath. He had no legs and he was depending upon me for strength. In all my life I had never had to lift a man in and out of a bath. Such a simple thing to do, yet I was conscious that I had probably never done anything more important. The people I was meeting were the ones with dignity and humour and it made my vanity and self-preoccupation look foolish. As I reflected upon their suffering and humility, I was growing up and learning about true strength.

In the evenings we would find ourselves gathered with loads of other hospital volunteers in a favourite French bar, singing the nights away until the early hours. The combination of hospital work, the example of the patients' faith, and the long raucous nights out with loads of wonderful young people was a huge eye-opener for me. This was truly broadening my horizons. It was unclear as to why, but it was not difficult for me to be happy here. I returned several years later to do a shift in that hospital.

Several weeks after the trip, we gathered in the presbytery with our curate to share our photos. It is hard to imagine now, but we had sent off our film cartridges to some distant printing company who returned the developed photos in a bright orange envelope accompanied by the negatives. Most photos we took were rubbish, either out of focus or showing a large thumb print on the lens obliterating part of the subject. There were no mobile phones with cameras. Just plastic click-and-go cameras. Here we were, gathered around a large oak dining table, laughing at the pictures we had taken and their stories.

A knock on the door interrupted the laughter. The priest made his way to the door and opened it to reveal Joey, a well-known homeless man who spent his life walking the roads of south Leicestershire. "Joey," said the priest, as if he was pleased to see him. He wasn't. We'd chatted about this before. The problem churches face is that if they provide money or food for someone, they create a dependency. People return again and again, until a queue forms which the priests are not able to supply. The advice is to support professionally run shelters rather than attend to people directly, many of whom have mental health problems. Yet confronted by poverty, it is hard to turn your back on it. So with skill our priest attended to the man with genuine respect.

"What can I do for you, Joey?" he asked with a big smile.

"Hello, Father," said Joey. "I have no money Father, and I need some money."

"Now, Joey," Father replied, looking a little more serious, "what would you be needing the money for?"

By now the stench of alcohol was reaching us. The poor man smelt as though he had been sweating lager inside the same old clothes for years. Unsurprised by the question, Joey lifted his foot to reveal an upper shoe with no sole. "I need new shoes."

The man's foot could be seen through several holes in his sock and his shoe was pretty useless.

"What size are you, Joey?" asked the priest.

"I'm a ten," Joey replied.

"You are in luck today," said the priest, "I'm a ten too." Then he proceeded to take off a fine pair of black Italian shoes and give them to Joey.

At first Joey was stumped. He didn't want shoes, he wanted money. Then, as even he saw there was nothing else he could do, he took the shoes and proceeded to try them on.

"They're smart, Father," he said. "Very smart," and then he pretended to tap dance. He was pleased with the prospect of walking more comfortably.

"Thank you, Father," I heard him shout from the presbytery gate.

Our curate returned to us at the table as if nothing much had happened. We continued flipping through the photographs. I didn't. I was spellbound, deeply moved. "I want to be like that," I thought to myself.

At seventeen, I'd observed something – an act of kindness which struck me powerfully. I'd witnessed a combination of love and wisdom acting out of a person spontaneously, without an ulterior motive. It moved me deeply because unbeknown to the priest, I was witnessing in him an image of Christ at work. As a young man with answers of my own, I wasn't good at listening. For all the many sermons that man gave, I remember none of them, except only one: the day he gave away his shoes – and it has stayed with me ever since.

Making connections

At the time of Jesus, despite the message of the prophets, God was still understood as essentially remote from the people. God could be found somewhere in the thunder on Mount Sinai or behind the veil in the inner sanctuary of the Temple. The idea that God might become part of us, possess our lives, be the very breath we breathe was something they found difficult to understand or believe. "It is no longer I who live," St Paul told the Galatians, "but it is Christ who lives in me." This language of indwelling features strongly in John's Gospel; "Abide in me as I abide in you," says Jesus.

In declaring himself the "true vine" Jesus is speaking of this intimacy. The consequence of this indwelling is fruitfulness, vivid expressions of God's love in the choices we make: "Because apart from me you can do nothing."

For a brief moment I saw Christ in the priest's expression of mercy for the homeless man. The righteousness of that moment struck me deeply, enough for me to want to imitate what I saw. Although the priest would never have known it, God was reaching me through an action which came naturally to him. It was no big deal to him. That is part of why it was so remarkable. That moment and this story were the fruits of his action. Once you see it, you start looking for it. Once you start looking for it, you see it everywhere. All it takes is a simple pair of shoes and the prompting of the Holy Spirit, and before you know it, Christ is present.

Conversation starters

- When has someone's actions struck you as profoundly right or just?
- In what way might this be a sign of God at work in or among us?

Chapter 12

Decreasing

Now a discussion about purification arose between John's disciples and a Jew. They came to John and said to him, "Rabbi, the one who was with you across the Jordan, to whom you testified, here he is baptising, and all are going to him." John answered, "No one can receive anything except what has been given from heaven. You yourselves are my witnesses that I said, 'I am not the Messiah, but I have been sent ahead of him.' He who has the bride is the bridegroom. The friend of the bridegroom, who stands and hears him, rejoices greatly at the bridegroom's voice. For this reason my joy has been fulfilled. He must increase, but I must decrease."

John 3:25-30

Here are two stories – one about a fictitious hero who never lived, and the other about a real-life hero who did live.

In 1962 Harry Saltzman and Albert Broccoli produced the film *Dr No*. It was a screenplay of a novel by Ian Fleming based on the adventures of a British secret agent called James Bond. James Bond was sold to the world as, "What every woman wants and what every man wants to be." At the time of writing this, the twenty-fourth sequel is in the making. As a boy these films provided a wonderful alternative to a grey Saturday afternoon. As I grew up my imagination was filled with colourful images of boat chases on the bayou, ski stunts in the Swiss Alps, nasty scarred baddies and their silent henchmen – and then there were all those beautiful girls. Born in the same year that the film was released, I have lived in the shadow of this heroic character all my life. There have been times when I'd loved to have been James Bond.

Sadly and somewhat pathetically, the boyhood aspiration has not entirely left me. There are five reasons for this. Firstly, James Bond enjoyed longevity. He never grew old. He would rejuvenate every three or four movies to maintain the appeal of the suave detective. The years have not put bags under his eyes or inclined him to slip both legs out of the car before he stands up. He doesn't heave a sigh when he gets out of a chair or need a pair of glasses to read the newspaper. He never says "Pardon?" because he didn't catch the instruction. Secondly, his life is free from conventional responsibilities. He doesn't have to pick up kids from the childminder or remember to buy a "Get well soon" card after his mother-in-law's cataract operation. He doesn't need to stay at home to receive a delivery or go to the local hardware store to buy wall screws. Thirdly, he is affluent. He doesn't have to check his bank statements. You never see him visiting his boss's secretary with a collection of receipts and a monthly expense claim. Fourthly, he doesn't have to go to meetings about health and safety procedures, risk assessments, or data protection. His work is too important to spend time filling in forms, going to blue-sky meetings or sending emails. Finally, there seems to be a life of sexual adventure without responsibility. James has to woo and bed the object of his desire but he doesn't have to meet her parents, sit in cars arguing over what he meant by a comment he made at the table, or be reminded that he doesn't listen properly. James Bond appeals to the boy in most boys.

The movies, affluence, influence, sexual attractiveness, and hanging out in exotic locations are not bad things in themselves – but if we begin to believe these are what a successful life looks like, our real lives can begin to feel disappointing. We can lose our sense of appreciation for what we have. There is something quite understandable and yet concerning about watching the contestants in TV talent shows pleading with voters not to send them home, craving the attention they get away from their familiar routines.

Another hero, William (Billy) McFadzean, was born in 1895. He grew up on the east side of Belfast. Educated at Belfast Trade Preparatory School he was a popular and lively boy. He was also a boy with restless energy. His school record included thirty reprimands for bad behaviour. Tall, athletic and strong, he was much happier out on the rugby pitch playing for Collegians RFC. By the summer of 1916 he had joined up to become Private McFadzean of the Royal Irish Rifles. In the spring of that year he crossed the channel to northern France and was positioned close to Thiepval woods in the notorious Somme Valley. It was his misfortune to be part of a tragic generation, just one sacrificed life in the most expensive assault on the Western Front. Ironically, he would never climb out of those deep trenches and engage the enemy alongside the others.

At sunrise on the morning of 1 July, Billy McFadzean was carrying grenades to the troops in the trenches shortly before the fateful signal to attack. Billy picked up a wooden box of mills grenades. Unknown to him the rope handle securing the box had frayed, and it broke. Twelve grenades spilled into the trench, the safety pins falling from some of them. It was not immediately clear which grenades had lost their pins. In a tightly packed trench filled with soldiers ready to attack, the effect of the blast would have been concentrated and devastating. Without hesitation Billy lay himself upon the spilt grenades. It was a spontaneous act of courage and love. Those who were there say that as he lay upon them, he had time to begin to sing "My Little Grey Home in the West". The explosion killed him instantly, but its full impact was smothered. As his comrades testified, he saved the lives of all those around him. His courage earned him the Victoria Cross, a medal which was presented to his father in Buckingham Palace.

Making connections

In this tiny passage from John's Gospel, we could be forgiven for missing a wonderful lesson. The narrative is so brief it is easy to overlook. The disciples of John the Baptist are unhappy. John has become a celebrity. By word of mouth and with no mass media to promote him, tens of thousands of people flock to hear him as he preaches from a ledge in the wilderness. John has the religious "X" factor. The crowds admire his charismatic teaching, his eccentric way of life, and his call to a new start. They queue up to be baptised by his disciples. What wonderful times for those closest to John, swept up by an atmosphere of fervour, urgency and significance.

For John's disciples these were the halcyon days. Yet despite being those closest to John, they had understood little of his prophetic message. Collectively, which is important (this is a planned meeting), they come to John with a complaint. The one to whom John had been referring to, that is Jesus, was attracting John's followers away from him. In only a few words their disappointment and envy are tangible.

John does not regard himself as a celebrity. He clearly understands his purpose. He is here to prepare the way for another. Having greeted and baptised Jesus, John knows that his mission is achieved and then he tells us, "For this reason my joy has been fulfilled. He must increase, but I must decrease." There is a beautiful piece of wisdom for us here, and one which can help us avoid a great deal of pain or the prospect of causing it.

Most of us have lived or are living through a necessary and enjoyable time of ambition. Ambition is not a bad thing. We are driven with a desire to be successful, to make an impact in some way, to be recognised and appreciated. It drives many of us through making our life decisions. During this time we choose our partners, identify a vocation, and anticipate a future. We want to change the world around us and in different ways we believe we can. This is what the author Ronald Rolheiser refers to as "essential discipleship". We prize the significance of our own contribution. We teach our young people to be essential disciples, to go for it, to make a difference, to go beyond the mediocre, and all of this is indeed a good message.

Eventually, though, the desire to be appreciated stops working. The idea of being the best won't satisfy. Staying the best is even harder. Eventually we continue to seek significance but not in the ways we once thought important. From wanting to be successful we begin to desire the success of others – our children, perhaps, or our friends. Slowly we decrease, as John decreased, not in our preciousness to God or each other, but in our efforts to be impressive. As Mother Teresa taught her congregation, "Our lives are not about us." What sounds like a difficult lesson is in fact immensely liberating and the source of John's joy. We no longer have to prove ourselves because, like John at the river's edge, we have encountered Jesus. There is real freedom here.

James Bond the fictional hero is impressive in all the ways we think we should be. He makes good decisions, defeats his enemies, enjoys the admiration of his peers and wins the girl. Billy McFadzean is a genuine hero, who recognised the value of the people he stood alongside, and saw that in the fulfilment of his life was a sacrifice for theirs. Billy had nothing to gain. Our lives are in many ways a necessary journey from the impressive to the sacrificial. We move from being the centre of our own lives to desiring the best for others. People who learn this earlier have a tendency to be happier.

There is nothing quite as strange as seeing an older person desperately acting out of the James Bond school of significance. What works for the young makes us look foolish in later life, not just because we get slower, but because wisdom moves us toward a more generous place. We slowly move away from the centre of our own lives. The alternative is not to grow up, and in an older body, James Bond looks silly.

Conversation starters

- What do you think causes people to have a mid-life crisis?
- In what ways has your understanding of success matured?

Chapter 13

17, Holloway Street

And so the kingdom of Heaven may be compared to a king who decided to settle his accounts with his servants. When the reckoning began, they brought him a man who owed ten thousand talents; he had no means of paying, so his master gave orders that he should be sold, together with his wife and children and all his possessions, to meet the debt. At this, the servant threw himself down at his master's feet, with the words, "Be patient with me and I will pay the whole sum." And the servant's master felt so sorry for him that he let him go and cancelled the debt. Now as this servant went out, he happened to meet a fellow-servant who owed him one hundred denarii; and he seized him by the throat and began to throttle him, saying, "Pay what you owe me." His fellow-servant fell at his feet and appealed to him, saying, "Be patient with me and I will pay you." But the other would not agree; on the contrary, he had him thrown into prison till he should pay the debt. His fellow-servants were deeply distressed when they saw what had happened, and they went to their master and reported the whole affair to him. Then the master sent for the man and said to him, "You wicked servant, I cancelled all that debt of yours when you appealed to me. Were you not bound, then, to have pity on your fellow-servant just as I had pity on you?" And in his anger the master handed him over to the torturers till he should pay all his debt. And that is how my heavenly Father will deal with you unless you each forgive your brother from your heart.

Matthew 18:23-35

I t was five days after Christmas 1942, a bright sunny morning by all accounts, a bit on the chilly side. At about 12.30pm at 17 Holloway Street in Exeter, Frances Brown was preparing lunch with her two grandchildren, Fred, who was nine, and Christopher, who was just two years old. The routine was interrupted by the piercing sound of the sirens alerting them to an impending air raid.

The three of them huddled together waiting for the danger to pass. It didn't. The bomb which landed close to their house was the last bombing raid to beset their city, one of a handful of hit-and-run sorties by German bombers. The planes flew fast and low up the Exe estuary carrying 500kg high-explosive bombs for maximum devastation. The house, along with several neighbouring homes all densely packed together, collapsed into heaps of rubble, timber and glass.

Frances and her grandchildren were trapped beneath huge piles of bricks and mortar. Reports indicate that their rescue came too late to save them. As you drive along that busy stretch of road today all that remains is a short unimpressive stretch of tarmac on the journey to work, where traffic queues towards traffic lights on the inner ring road. You could never imagine that it was once a scene of such tragedy and loss. How quickly our efforts to tidy up conceal scenes of past suffering. There are places like 17 Holloway Street in most cities – places that you would never know existed.

Strangely this all began with a tourist guide. In 1940, a German plane deployed to attack industrial targets discharged its bombs over London before returning home. Historians generally agree that the incident was a mistake. Bombers often discharged the remaining payload of bombs in order to increase the speed of their return. The British Government believed this to be an attack on civilian homes and it marked a new level of depravity. The Royal Air Force retaliated with an attack on Berlin. Both sides believed that to attack civilian homes would break the morale of people and bring about capitulation. The devastation of city streets on both sides of the English Channel escalated, especially in Germany where the combined allied assault wreaked almost total destruction of several cities.

On the 28 March 1942, 234 British bombers attacked Lübeck, the Hanseatic fishing port on the Baltic coast of Germany. A thousand people died. The attack incensed Hitler, not because of the fatalities, but because the city was a beautiful timber-structured medieval place of quaint narrow streets and pretty little squares. The timber buildings were consumed by spreading fires. For Hitler, destroying this jewel of German heritage was an attack on the nation's cultural identity. The devastation was something he could not tolerate and he quickly ordered reprisal attacks on historic targets in England. He went after the cathedrals, cloisters and castles of England.

The first of these raids was on Exeter in late April 1942. The next day the German propagandist, Gustav Braun von Sturm, declared: "We shall go out and bomb every building in Britain marked with three stars in the Baedeker Guide." The Baedeker Guide was the world's most famous tourist guide, translated into many languages and popular across Western Europe. What was once the means to appreciate and enjoy foreign culture now became a blueprint for demolition. Exeter was to be bombed, not as a city of industry or munitions, but because like Lübeck it was quaint and historic. Exeter would become a victim of its own beauty.

On 23 April the first of nineteen German bombing raids on Exeter took place. Similar attacks on York, Bath, Norwich and Canterbury were designed to destroy architectural heritage and with it, a sense of national pride. In total the raids, which became known as the "Baedecker Raids", destroyed over fifty thousand homes, killing 1,637 civilians. Ernst Von Kugel, a German pilot in the Exeter raids said: "We thought of our Führer and the command he gave, 'revenge.'"

Today, if you walk along the High Street in Exeter you come across strange configuration of buildings. The Guildhall, dated 1590, and cloth-merchants' houses built in 1650, stand alongside concrete buildings erected after the War, a disjointed architectural scene. Different centuries of architectural history are squeezed alongside, behind and in front, in an incongruous mixture. It has left the High Street with a series of urban scars, reminders of terrible violence.

For Frances Brown and her two grandchildren the escalation of reprisals and revenge marked the end of their lives. It would be hard to explain to the mother of Fred and Christopher that her family had died to avenge the destruction of some medieval buildings in Lübeck, but that is what happens when things escalate. We forget how it all started. On all sides, the unfortunate men and women whose job it was to recover the bodies were left wondering what manner of argument leads to the bombing of children in their homes.

Making connections

Getting our own back is remarkably appealing. Revenge has the feel of cancelling a wrong. We can quickly find ourselves caught up in such an escalation. On the surface of things the original "crime" might be something barely noticeable – a comment or a look. It usually starts with believing that someone doesn't like or respect us. Things have a habit of escalating until one day we are devoured by an urge to get even. It becomes all we think about to such an extent that we can't remember how it all began. Before we know it we are retaliating in kind, seeking allies, misinterpreting signals and fear develops a momentum of its own. In extreme cases the ultimate consequence is war.

There is no easy way to resolve this. At some stage we have to run against it, absorb the movement for reprisal, increase our stride, until we have stepped off the escalator. Someone at some stage has to take a hit and not return it in kind. This is why Jesus is so extraordinary. He did not accelerate the cycle of accusations and reprisals. He never acted out of a desire to cancel a debt by inflicting another.

In the Gospel passage Jesus is calling upon us to cancel the debt and let go of the urge to exact revenge. A man is released from his debt, but it doesn't lead him to gratitude and mercy. Instead he seeks vengeance on those who are indebted to him. This story is not about money. We hold people to account for the wrongs they have done against us. We refuse to let go of the hurt they caused. In this way we remain indebted to them, resentfully seeking the last word.

In the story, the price we pay for being forgiven is to forgive, to be courageous enough to absorb some of the pain we have experienced and not return it with interest. This is not the same as accepting abuse, which affirms the abuser and confines a person to the role of victim.

What makes our saints saintly is not a form of angelic purity or some otherworldly disposition lacking any humour, but the insatiable urge to run against the desire to get even. The saints ran down the up escalator, the opposite to what happened at 17 Holloway Street. If the victims of bombing throughout the world could speak to us from their place of tragedy, they would call us to run down the upward escalator, to absorb the desire to inflict pain on others, otherwise all of us will one day finish up buried in the rubble of our disputes.

Spare a thought for Gordon Wilson and his daughter Marie. On 8 November 1987, Gordon lay beneath the rubble caused by a bomb planted in Enniskillen by the IRA. Holding tightly the hand of his twenty-year-old daughter Marie, who lay wounded by his side, she said faintly, "I love you Daddy," shortly before she died. Within hours of being rescued, Gordon was broadcast all over the world by the BBC insisting, "I bear no ill will. I bear no grudge... I will pray for these men tonight and every night." It was one of the greatest acts of courage and resilience I have ever seen and his call for reconciliation became a defining moment in the journey to peace.

Conversation starters

- When do we notice the desire to get even?
- How might we cancel the debt we hold others to?

Chapter 14

The sheep dip

Then the people of Jerusalem and all Judea were going out to him, and all the region along the Jordan, and they were baptised by him in the river Jordan, confessing their sins. But when he saw many Pharisees and Sadducees coming for baptism, he said to them, "You brood of vipers! Who warned you to flee from the wrath to come? Bear fruit worthy of repentance. Do not presume to say to yourselves, 'We have Abraham as our ancestor'; for I tell you, God is able from these stones to raise up children to Abraham. Even now the axe is lying at the root of the trees; every tree therefore that does not bear good fruit is cut down and thrown into the fire. I baptise you with water for repentance, but one who is more powerful than I is coming after me; I am not worthy to carry his sandals. He will baptise you with the Holy Spirit and fire. His winnowing-fork is in his hand, and he will clear his threshing floor and will gather his wheat into the granary; but the chaff he will burn with unquenchable fire." Then Jesus came from Galilee to John at the Jordan, to be baptised by him. John would have prevented him, saying, "I need to be baptised by you, and do you come to me?" But Jesus answered him, "Let it be so now; for it is proper for us in this way to fulfil all righteousness." Then he consented. And when Jesus had been baptised, just as he came up from the water, suddenly the heavens were opened to him and he saw the Spirit of God descending like a dove and alighting on him. And a voice from heaven said, "This is my Son, the Beloved, with whom I am well pleased."

Matthew 3:5-17

In early autumn 1962, in a quiet little market town somewhere in the middle of England, a group of adults gathered together to baptise me. From what others tell me it was an unremarkable day. Light rain, grey skies, a Sunday morning with a hint of what would become an extremely cold winter. My mother had not recovered from giving birth and was anaemic and exhausted. My dad was tired out from long shifts in the construction industry. My godparents bought for me the usual prayer books and a silver spoon but I barely saw them again. The priest was in a bit of a hurry, caught between presiding at Mass and another appointment. Meanwhile I slept through it all. This small group of faithful people huddled around a font near the church door one Sunday afternoon. They prayed for me as I was baptised.

Like most baptisms, mine didn't make the news. A group of tired adults pouring water onto the head of an unconscious two-month-old baby. What possible significance could this have? One might ask – given the dramatic events which were going on in the world at the time, and the stresses and worries in the lives of those people – why on earth did they bother?

In East Devon, situated between the Exe estuary and the River Otter, lies Woodbury Common. I love being there, and I have spent hours walking and running its myriad paths. The landscape is made up of pebble beds deposited there two hundred million years ago by a vast river. With little in the way of soil, the result is a rutted landscape of sand, stones, heath, gorse and heathers, interrupted by the occasional woodland copse and hardy tree plantations. The whole common is criss-crossed with tiny paths in the undergrowth and bridleways which cut deep into the pebbles, forming paths in dry weather and gullies after a storm.

The seasons are vivid on the common. Whether walking through the fresh tall grasses of spring, the yellow and purple gorse bushes of summer, the rich orange decay of autumn, or the sparse sleeping winter landscape, the common is a great escape, a timeless, tranquil, unassuming sort of place. It is a place to be yourself, and to do some thinking.

The common whispers. If you listen, you can hear the people who have walked there before. For such a remote place it has played its part in history. It was the home of an industrious Iron Age community who built a hill fort there. It was the site of a vicious battle in 1549, a prelude to a massacre in a nearby village. In the Second World War it provided shelter for hundreds of US troops who hid there in preparation for the invasion of Normandy. As you take the paths across the common, you come across remnants of their activities – oddly sited abandoned brickwork and unnaturally level parade grounds hint of a more hectic time. In the spring of 1944, the common was far from being a place of solitude.

Nearby Lympstone is home to the Royal Marines' Commando Training Centre. If you are walking on Woodbury Common it is not unusual for the tranquillity which characterises this area to be shattered by a platoon of soldiers running past fully camouflaged, carrying machine guns. The earth is riddled with tread marks from the boots of exhausted trainees who, in order to earn the green beret, must spend hours in rigorous training both day and night. Occasionally out walking you might come across a rope to guide the trainees through a bog, or a tunnel for them to crawl through. You would barely notice them unless you were shown them.

Early one morning I was on the common with the dog. It was a mild November morning, but grey. Very grey. Winter had arrived, the autumn storms had cleared the trees of their leaves and the ground had lost its vivid autumn carpet. The many bogs and puddles captured and held the rain and mirrored the low cloud cover. The only busyness on the common was in the streams and gullies draining away the storm water. It was the time of year when the paths were more visible, like varicose veins. Through depleted vegetation the red sand and pale pebbles provided a bit of colour. But for that and the evergreen pine trees, the common had gone into a state of deep sleep.

My solitude that morning was starkly interrupted. Well into my walk and heading down one of the valley sides I suddenly heard aggressive shouting, swearing, and then cheering. It could only be the Marines on a training exercise. From among the gorse bushes I arrived at a clearing in the hillside and there they were, an entire unit of trainees lined up, breathing fast. Unlike me, they had no time to admire their surroundings, their minds were set on completing an endurance challenge.

Before them were two concrete pits dug into the ground and filled to the brim with thick black murky water fed by a stream. Connecting the two pits was a concrete culvert completely hidden under water. The recruits were ordered to stand in the water and submerge themselves to crawl through the culvert and then reappear in the neighbouring pit. A fellow recruit stood in the pit opposite, ready to help pull each one out. It is not a long culvert, about two metres in length, but it was deep enough and long enough to make it an act of courage, an adrenalin rush. Although underwater only briefly, when each reappeared they were gasping for breath and briefly disorientated. Then with the challenge behind them they would continue the run, past me and up the path I had just come down. They were drenched but not cold, gasping for breath but focused on carrying on.

A few recruits found the prospect of the culvert, known as the "sheep dip", a real challenge. Holding back one or two others to help, the officers began to intensify their shouts of encouragement. Pumping them up, the prospect of not completing the task was becoming too much, and one by one the few remaining recruits overcame their fear and quite literally took the plunge, emerging to the sound of cheers. It was not difficult to admire these young people, completing a challenge they obviously found terrifying.

Left alone on the hillside, the noise and spectacle over, there was something about this challenge that really intrigued me. I took a closer look. The black pools of water were placid now, belying their more sinister purpose. Later, while chatting to a Marine friend I asked about the purpose of the murky "sheep dip".

"Well," he said, "it's like all these sort of things; you learn to trust the people who put you there, and you do it, and you leave your fear behind in the water."

Wouldn't it be good, I thought, if in life you could go down into the water and come up on the other side free of the things that make you unhappy or incapable? That is exactly what happens on a hillside in Woodbury Common. When Emily my daughter did the sheep dip challenge at an event run by the Marines she said quite casually, "Yeah, you come up out of the water and its nothing really. I'd do it again." That wasn't how she felt shortly before she did it. It is all about coming up out of the water without the fear and reluctance you had going into it.

Making connections

It is tempting to read the abrasive and uncompromising speech of John the Baptist's as a rebuff of some people and not others. The chaff or weeds will die and only the wheat will be left. This speech though, applies to each of us. John was baptising with water, reinforcing the Judaic tradition of washing away sinfulness in preparation for coming into the presence of God. The people he preached to would have understood the symbolism. In this passage, in almost apocalyptic language, he takes it further.

Everything that separates us from God will be burned away like the impurities in iron ore. John's baptism washes from the outside. Jesus' baptism purifies from the inside. While our bodies are submerged and washed, a fire burns in the heart of us, consuming everything that generates fear and selfishness.

Through baptism God now resides not on the outside, but on the inside of our lives.

The early Christians understood this and emphasised it in the baptism ritual. After agreeing to be baptised, it was common to be submerged, literally pushed down into the water three times, in the name of the Father, the Son and the Holy Spirit. Each time you would surface straining for air to inflate your lungs. It would be as if you were breathing for the first time, born again. Your old earthly life, motivated by the needs of self, had to die so that you could rise up out of the waters to a new life. As Paul taught in his letter to the Romans, "we have been buried with him by baptism into death, so that, just as Christ was raised from the dead by the glory of the Father, so we too might walk in newness of life." This is the power of going down into the water.

For Christians, baptism is an immense once-and-for-all never-to-be-repeated moment. When the Christian community accepted babies for baptism, it was deemed too dangerous to start throwing them into rivers. So the ritual was changed and water was poured more carefully onto the baby's head. It began to lose some of its visual power. We began to lose some of what I saw on Woodbury Common. Like the Marines, we too have to trust the people who brought us to this moment and leave our outside dirt and inner fears behind in the water. Slowly our lives will bring us to a complete freedom, especially if we learn not to forget that sheep dip moment.

Conversation starters

- If you are baptised, what do you know about your own baptism?
- What do you think about being submerged at baptism?
- How might it help us to stay tuned to and remember our baptism?

Chapter 15

Beware the hero inside

He also told this parable to some who trusted in themselves that they were righteous and regarded others with contempt: "Two men went up to the temple to pray, one a Pharisee and the other a tax-collector. The Pharisee, standing by himself, was praying thus, 'God, I thank you that I am not like other people: thieves, rogues, adulterers, or even like this tax-collector. I fast twice a week; I give a tenth of all my income.' But the tax-collector, standing far off, would not even look up to heaven, but was beating his breast and saying, 'God, be merciful to me, a sinner!' I tell you, this man went down to his home justified rather than the other; for all who exalt themselves will be humbled, but all who humble themselves will be exalted."

Luke 18:9-14

When I got on the train at Manchester Piccadilly there was plenty of room. Four seats and a table all to myself. Pulling out the contents of my briefcase I began to write up the scribbled notes I had made during the day's meeting. As the train accelerated out of the station I was distracted by the view from the window. The train line sliced its way through the urban sprawl. The view from the window offered a cross-section of who we all are, a split-second glimpse into the way we live. The tiny little flats, the congested rear yards of the Victorian terraces, and then the suburbs with the proliferation of conservatories and garden trampolines. Soon we were heading beyond the city and into the patchwork quilt of greens and yellows which make up the rural landscape.

Travelling has always stimulated me. Every view arouses fresh curiosity. My job of writing up the minutes was not proceeding very quickly. There was too much to enjoy. Neither did I notice the gradual accumulation of passengers as the train made its way from town to town towards Langley Mill near Nottingham. The man now sitting opposite me brought out what looked like a report. He was examining it carefully, making notes in the margin as he did so. He was wearing a dark charcoal suit. His watch, his pen, his briefcase all had the look of items which had been chosen carefully. He gave the impression of success. He was someone serious. Something about him made me feel uneasy. He approached his paperwork with commendable concentration. He looked like he would never be distracted by a view from the window. Perhaps I should be more like him?

Next to me was another man dressed similarly to the man opposite. He was another businessman, looking at a sheet of tiny figures in columns. He was tapping away on his calculator. He was older, plump, fighting a losing battle with food. Neither of these men sharing my table had any sense of what was around them. There was no looking up and beyond their paperwork. They were both living in a tiny space between themselves and the work they had to do.

"Is this what professionalism looks like?" I asked myself. "Is this how I should be?"

When they arrived home they would probably relax, while I would have to get out my unfinished work because of all the distractions around me. I was troubled by my lack of concentration.

The fourth seat at our table was taken by a younger woman. I marvelled at her flexibility. She took off her shoes and squeezed one leg beneath the other. Sitting like that she looked more at home than the rest of us, as if she were sitting on a sofa. She spent a while investigating her headphones and then scrambling inside her bag, pulling out a bottle of water and a paperback. I was struck by the fact that all four of us had acknowledged one another's presence, yet we were definitely avoiding any further communication. My three companions were now firmly in their own worlds. So I returned to mine and the view out of the window. What a strange world we live in, so close and yet so far apart.

Gathering around us now were all sorts of people. The train had stopped several times and the carriage had become crowded. It was late afternoon and many of these people were heading home from work. People were standing in the aisle.

Accelerating out of yet another station our individual bubbles were pierced by a piercing cry. In the aisle next to our table a young woman was cradling a distressed baby. The child only paused to inhale, before emitting another outburst. I glanced in her direction and offered a smile. She had no time for such pleasantries. Appealing for her attention was another child, his arms extended upwards expectantly, as if to demand that she pick him up. It looked terribly stressful. She cradled the baby with one arm while trying to reach into her bag with the other. The boy was pulling on her skirt. She pulled out a biscuit to placate him. As she did so the folded buggy propped up against her leg fell over and the bag over her shoulder slipped down her arm.

In such a tiny space the woman was trying to carry a crying child, entertain a second, carry a bag of shopping and balance a folded pram. Despite her predicament, my fellow passengers and I continued in our own self-absorption. The girl next to me was tapping her book to the rhythm of the music she was listening to.

My business companions were not even briefly distracted from their work. It is remarkable that we respond to disruption as if it weren't happening at all. Despite her distress, the mother was ignored, avoided, left to her own problems.

I'm not sure how long it took me before I stood up and appealed to her to take my seat. It was a welcome gesture.

"Thank you, thank you," she repeated. "It is so embarrassing," she said, and pointing to the tearful infant explained that she was teething.

Sitting down she felt more protected from the glances of her fellow travellers. "I'm off at the next station" she explained. "You can have your seat back then."

"No need," I said. "I'm getting off too."

As she regained her composure I could see that she was stressed by the unwanted attention that a distressed child generates. By now, her little boy was smearing the melted chocolate off his fingers onto the hem of her skirt. She put some gel on her finger and rubbed it onto the gum of her baby who was temporarily consoled. Apart from adjusting the position of his briefcase on the table, no one else seemed to recognise this woman's predicament.

The train was pulling into the station. I could see more people standing outside waiting to add to the pressure in the carriage.

"Please," I said, "let me help," and reaching out I picked up the folded buggy and offered to carry the shopping.

"Excuse us," I say loudly, in order to exit the carriage, but with a hint of admonishment.

I wanted to disturb the commuters' collective indifference. With my briefcase and her things in hand, the mother was free to guide her little boy and carry her baby.

"Excuse us," I said again, so that we could exit the carriage.

As we stood on the platform I turned to her and with a heavy sigh apologised for everyone's indifference.

"Isn't it terrible what commuting does to people?" I said. "I'm sure they wouldn't normally be like that. But I suppose that if you do it every day you learn to switch off from each other."

"No harm done," she replied, unfolding the buggy and positioning her baby in the seat. "We'll soon be home. Thank you again," she said, smiling for the first time as she took her shopping and proceeded towards the car park.

As the train left the station I was pleased to be out of the confines of such a crowded space. It was a hot and stuffy evening to be on a crowded train. Briefly, I congratulated myself for being big enough to see the plight of someone else.

"I'm glad I'm not like one of those zombies," I thought.

It was only then that it dawned on me that the car park in the train station was in the wrong place, as was the station ticket office. Indeed, there was a road bridge over the railway line that shouldn't have been there. Damn, this wasn't my station. I'd got off in the wrong place. As I walked into the car park the woman I had helped was being greeted by a friend. I managed to acquire one of the waiting taxis. The train was now fast disappearing beyond the station.

"Follow that train," I said to the taxi driver, as if I was in a chase movie.

The driver laughed. "How do you get off a train at the wrong station?" he asked, seeing the stupidity of what I had just done.

"By being stuck in your own world," I said ironically.

Serves me right.

Making connections

It is easy to glance over the parable of the Pharisee and the tax collector and think we know what it's all about. The lesson looks too obvious. We imagine that we don't tend to look down on people, and because many of us battle with our confidence (or lack of it) we don't consciously assert ourselves as better than others. That is true for most of us, most of the time, until we see behaviours in others that we dislike. At which point we can slip into imagining we are above such things. The Pharisee's excuse for exalting himself is that he sees things in others that he hates. From his observation and judgement of others he is able to imagine that because he sees it, he wouldn't fall for it himself.

The warning in the passage is to beware of the risk of self-praise and the delusion it provokes. In the end we will all learn the importance of humility, but it may have to be learned through tough circumstance. Back on the train between Manchester and Nottingham I was quite happy in my own world, admiring the beauty of the landscape. When others became lost inside their own worlds I became condemning and self-congratulating. I found my own reward in coming to the aid of a fellow traveller. Here was I, showing these people that I am not like them. I'm better than them. For T.S Eliot the final temptation is to do the right thing for the wrong reason. This is not good. This is me, doing the right thing for the wrong reason.

Our merciful God, whose ways are so above ours, knows that what I needed was an abrupt lesson in my own stupidity, and once again that is what I got. As I stood on that platform I could hear a thousand saints laughing their heads off.

Conversation starters

- What is humility and where do we notice it?
- What does it mean to be taught a lesson in humility and has that ever happened to you?

Chapter 16

Growing pains

When they had finished breakfast, Jesus said to Simon Peter, "Simon son of John, do you love me more than these?" He said to him, "Yes, Lord; you know that I love you." Jesus said to him, "Feed my lambs." A second time he said to him, "Simon son of John, do you love me?" He said to him, "Yes, Lord; you know that I love you." Jesus said to him, "Tend my sheep." He said to him the third time, "Simon son of John, do you love me?" Peter felt hurt because he said to him the third time, "Do you love me?" And he said to him, "Lord, you know everything; you know that I love you." Jesus said to him, "Feed my sheep. Very truly, I tell you, when you were younger, you used to fasten your own belt and to go wherever you wished. But when you grow old, you will stretch out your hands, and someone else will fasten a belt around you and take you where you do not wish to go." (He said this to indicate the kind of death by which he would glorify God.) After this he said to him, "Follow me." Peter turned and saw the disciple whom Jesus loved following them; he was the one who had reclined next to Jesus at the supper and had said, "Lord, who is it that is going to betray you?" When Peter saw him, he said to Jesus, "Lord, what about him?" Jesus said to him, "If it is my will that he remain until I come, what is that to you? Follow me!"

John 21:15-22

When the children were little they would look to us to invent games for them. We'd pretend the carpet was molten lava and try and get around the house without touching the floor. Such games were easy because they could imagine it straight away. They'd trust the game immediately, expecting it to work. Another game involved trust rather than imagination.

As a boy, Sam would stand with his arms raised insistently. With two hands stretched to the sky he would wait for his entertainment. Carefully placing one hand underneath each armpit, with a sudden exertion I would throw him hard into the air. As a tiny little boy I could really propel him upwards. He could get so much height that it had to be a game for outdoors. As he reached that brief moment of weightlessness he would be looking down upon me. He wasn't thinking to himself "The poor old feller is looking a bit tired." The only word to come squealing out of his mouth would be "again!" As gravity returned him to me he would be longing for his next go. It would never have occurred to that little lad that his father might drop him. Perhaps this is what Jesus meant when he suggested that his learned listeners might become more like little children. Sam's faith in me was absolute and utterly humbling. In that moment it was impossible not to love him completely. I'd vow never to drop him.

That kind of trust has other expressions. As we were travelling down the motorway on a long journey Matthew was restless, somehow managing to overcome the sleepiness which had silenced his brother and sister.

"I'm bored," he said, kicking his legs the way kids do.

The motorway was long, straight and tedious. Alison and I were searching for ways to keep him occupied. We started to play a game in which he would try to guess the meaning of all the road signs. By the time we arrived at our destination two hours later, I was sick of explaining what every warning sign meant.

Later that night we were sitting around the kitchen table. Matt looked really worried, staring over his spaghetti bolognese.

"What is the matter?" I asked him.

With a sigh he asked heavily, "Dad, is it really true that tiredness can kill?"

As we had passed the sign encouraging us to call in at the motorway service station, he had taken my explanation of the sign as a literal truth. We had told him that we love him, we had told him that tiredness can kill. He believed both because of who was telling him. As he began to fight his tiredness, he was afraid that he would eventually die of it. There was no awareness of the need to apply, challenge it or contextualise the words.

Despite vowing to never drop my children, I did. Not intentionally or physically of course, but as a human I dropped them because I am not perfect. Part of growing up is to discover that our parents are not perfect. Another part of growing up is to discover that neither are we. My parents didn't turn out to be perfect, and neither did I. So what is to trust?

One day that little child walks down the stairs a teenager. I have met countless parents who despair at the loss of the child to the awkward door slammer who emerges from the bedroom one morning. Teenagers are not sure what to trust and so almost everything is worth kicking to see what it does under pressure. One woman told me how her daughter had put her through two solid years of torment.

"We tiptoed around our own house," she said, "for fear of offending our daughter, never sure whether we she wanted us dead or alive. One minute she hated me and wished she had younger parents and the next minute she was charming, asking me for a lift to her friend's house."

Finally after the strain had got too much she let her rage out. In an unguarded moment she released months of pent-up tension.

"I don't like you," she shouted at her daughter. "You deaden the atmosphere in our home and you make it miserable for everyone." Then she added, "But I love you, and I'll love you longer than you will keep doing this to us."

She described a silent and perplexed teenager who didn't quite know how to object to that.

An angst-ridden teenager will generally hold up what is being said by an authority figure and measure it against what is being practised – and if the two don't match, will exploit it to the full. Challenging is part of the teenager character.

For some people, faith has neither the character of the confident child, nor of the angry teenager. After an evening working in a small Plymouth parish, a parishioner asked if I would continue the conversation after the meeting we had just had. I sensed a little loneliness and agreed that the next time I was in town I would pay her a visit and we would talk some more. Her house was one of those splendid Victorian terraces whose frontage belies the much larger home behind it. The width of the house was little more than a door and a bay window and at the front was only a narrow garden. From a beautiful tiled corridor hallway she took me into the front room, which contained a glass cabinet with a few pieces of bone china and some cut glass. There was a large grey tiled fireplace with a pair of ornamental swans on either side, and a brass fireplace set with a little shovel and a brush. I sat on an olive-green sofa. The bay window behind me was adorned with thick net curtains that dulled the light. The room was pristine but slightly musty. I was reminded of many houses like this I had visited as a child. The older generation reserves a best room in the front of the house for important visitors like priests or doctors. We had a pot of tea with a tea strainer.

As we talked I became aware of a sound coming from the kitchen and I realised we were not alone. There was the sound of a squeaky cupboard. As we talked my hostess suddenly bellowed, "What are you looking for?" I nearly dropped my bone china cup.

A muffled male voice replied, "Nothing."

There was a long silence before she shouted again, "It is in the end cupboard underneath the bread bin." The conversation made no sense whatsoever.

It occurred to me that here was another kind of faith. There was something here that lacked logic or sequence but was very relational. The woman's husband denied looking for the biscuits she told him not to eat, even though she bought them for him and told him where she had hidden them.

"They are bad for him," she said, justifying herself, having bought them in the first place.

It makes sense if you have been together for a long time and learned to live with the very things you can't change. Here were two people who had a language all of their own. As they insulted each other, I was aware how little the insults penetrated. The rules of engagement no longer seemed to matter to this couple, they had outlived the language of rights and regulations and now possessed a profound love. They are so together that death will seem cruel, but they have life now, and have it to the full.

Making connections

We mostly associate maturity with losing our childishness. We put our "childish ways" behind us, as St Paul tells us. Maturity though, is more than something associated with age. Church wisdom suggests that faith is also a process of growing up, maturing with every other aspect of our lives. If we remain open to the promptings of the Spirit we will continue throughout our lives to grow up. Growth in maturity doesn't stop when we leave school.

Sometimes we are like the child enjoying times of certainty and clarity, with absolute trust in the law and lawgiver. We can with confident trust fall into the loving arms of a father because we do not doubt in his ability to catch us. Our shouting is for more. In these times we are like the centurion in Matthew's Gospel who tells Jesus, "Only say the word and my servant will be healed." He doesn't need evidence. He simply needs the instruction. His faith is resolute.

Sometimes we are the young girl questioning and testing her family, challenging the love that is offered because she doesn't really love herself. We want to challenge what is there, understand it better and if necessary kick it a bit to see if it is what it claims to be. In these moments we are Thomas provoking outrage by insisting that we won't believe until we can put our finger in the scar the spear made. We can't trust it until we have evidence. Sometimes we are the wisdom figures, having grown through times of difficulty and doubt. We have given up the desire to control what is ultimately in God's hands. We are provoked more by an encounter of meeting love than understanding it. By learning to surrender into a certain mystery we have begun to laugh at ourselves and to make the prayer of Jesus' truly our own, "Thy will be done."

Despite linking these growing pains to physical maturity, the reality is that they are all needed at different times, and all three help us to grow up in one way or another. In the scripture passage Jesus indicates the kind of death by which Peter will "glorify God", but there is something richer here for us all. There will be a time when should our faith mature with us, we will no longer depend on the law, or upon evidence and understanding, but will with growing wisdom learn to accept the loss of our own self-determination. Following Peter's declaration of love for Jesus, there emerges the direction he must now take. Gradually he will learn not to rely upon his own strength but on the will of the

Father. Despite being captured and led where he does not wish to go, he will be truly free. Free from his own struggle to be in control, a desire which would only demonstrate his limitations. He will in time stretch out his hands and give in to God's love for him, no matter where it takes him. That destiny is ours too.

Conversation starters

- With which of the three types of faith do you most identify: the child falling into his father's arms, the teenager protesting with questions, or the couple's abstract conversation through a brick wall?
- How has your faith changed over the years? Do you think it is growing up?

Chapter 17

The apprentice

For this very reason, you must make every effort to support your faith with goodness, and goodness with knowledge, and knowledge with self-control, and self-control with endurance, and endurance with godliness, and godliness with mutual affection, and mutual affection with love. For if these things are yours and are increasing among you, they keep you from being ineffective and unfruitful in the knowledge of our Lord Jesus Christ. For anyone who lacks these things is short-sighted and blind, and is forgetful of the cleansing of past sins.

2 Peter 1:5-9

Every now and again we come into contact with our limitations. Jack did that for us. After four years of teaching him we were close to running out of strategies. Occasionally he would lose his temper. Because he was tall and strong he could be intimidating. By the time he reached his sixteenth birthday he was becoming unpredictable. Several teachers were nervous around him. Some felt unsafe teaching him. Jack, like so many students with behavioural issues, found school confusing. He couldn't cope with a lot of the work and was confronted daily by his own limitations. School for him was something of a humiliation. It was not easy to come last in tests again and again. After a while you learn to live with the idea that you are stupid.

During one lesson he pinned a classmate to the wall and a teacher from another classroom had to be sought in order to pull him away. It was becoming obvious that despite the patience of his tutor and the dedication of many teachers, it might be time to expel him. Expelling a student always feels like failure. No school expels a student happily, especially a student with learning difficulties. We did not want to cast him into the world like this with our task as yet unfinished.

As Head of Upper School it was my job, alongside his tutor and the school principal, to assess his situation. We invited his parents to the school to discuss his prospects. We gathered in the principal's office, his mother pleading his case.

"I know he is trouble," she said, ashamed of her own son, "but this school is all he has got."

His father sat with his head in his hands, staring at the floor. He didn't know what to say. It was all too painful. Holding him as a baby they would not have foreseen this. What had happened to their little boy, the one who climbed trees and had so much to say? It became obvious that his parents were defeated by his problems.

"He doesn't want to talk to us," they said. Unlike some parents we had interviewed in this situation, they didn't offer any excuses or blame other people. They blamed themselves. They were looking to us, and we to them. We all felt inadequate and unsure what was best for the boy and the school.

We summoned Jack to the office. All the most important adults in his life were in that room, looking for a resolution. He stood as he had done so many times before, wanting to please us and knowing at the same time that he had no real idea how to. He knew he had made many promises and broken them. In moments like this he was contrite and remorseful, his apology sincere. But he couldn't sustain his remorse beyond the first tease from a classmate. His rage came too quickly for him to rehearse a response and he knew it.

"Jack," the principal began, "we want to get you to leavers' day so that you can leave this school with your head held high instead of walking out now in shame. Do you want that?" Jack always wanted that. He liked being part of the school community, he just couldn't cope with the combination of authority and humiliation he experienced in lessons.

"Name the teachers you are most likely to work hard for," said the principal. Jack named his tutor and then to everyone's surprise he mentioned a second name, Andy. Andy was not a teacher, he was the manager of the site. He cleaned, repaired and secured the school. Andy was always in school early morning and late evening. Jack, who lived very near to the school, had struck up an unlikely friendship with this man.

Our caretaker had his own issues with authority. He did his job effectively but he didn't appreciate being around teachers. Whether they did or not, he felt that they looked down on him. He coped by doing what he was asked and nothing more. Asking him for help I'd say, "Andy, the door handle on my classroom is broken again, the kids have been swinging on it. Can you fix it for me?" "Yes, Mr Wells," he'd reply. "Andy, you can call me David," I'd insist. "Yes, Mr Wells," he'd reply. Although he had a smirk on his face, he also carried with him the idea that he was subordinate. So he insisted upon putting himself in that position. It was as if he preferred a distance between him and his colleagues. Andy had a way of appealing to some of the young people in the school who he thought were the bottom of the pile. Perhaps he saw himself in them.

Back in the office and after much careful thought and discernment a plan was hatched. Jack would spend each morning in the classroom with his tutor doing literacy and numeracy. In the afternoon he was assigned to shadow the caretaker. This would be his last chance. If the plan failed Jack would leave us prematurely without much hope of securing a place in another school. There were to be no more transgressions, no more moments of aggression.

It was remarkable how quickly the school became accustomed to the sight of the caretaker and Jack together. You'd see the older man, bin liner in hand, scooping up litter, and a few metres away Jack would be doing exactly the same. You'd see Andy, paintbrush in hand, instructing Jack how to hold the brush and paint up to the edges: "Don't overload the brush," he'd say, "or it'll drip down your hand." The next day you'd be leaving the school and there would be Andy and Jack together, clipping the hedge with trimmers. Little by little Jack would copy and then assume the skills of his master. Before long they were inseparable. Where ever you saw one you'd see the other, polishing floors, replacing lightbulbs, repairing door handles.

In search of Andy one day, I went to his office. It wasn't an office in the conventional sense; it was a long narrow room with whitewashed walls. There was a chair and desk and a dirty sink, a steam train calendar on the wall. The desk was hidden under paint pots, brushes, detergent packs, hosepipes, a mountain of toilet rolls and paper towels. The sink was home to a pile of stained and unwashed mugs. The floor was littered with pieces of equipment in various states of repair. Andy was always rebuilding something.

On this occasion though, I stood in the doorway speechless. They hadn't seen me peering into the room through a slightly open door. There were the two of them, a sixteen-year-old boy and a man almost four times his age, sitting side by side. On Jack's lap was a primary school reading book, the words in large print. There, in that small space, the caretaker was teaching the boy how to read, away from any risk of ridicule. By placing his trust in the caretaker, Jack too was playing his part, giving Andy a sense of his own worth. The two of them had become friends, offering each other dignity. My reason for going to his office escaped me now. I left it, whatever it was, and walked away. Whatever I needed could wait. In that little room was the solution to our problem.

Jack's mum bought him a suit for the leavers' prom. It was the first suit he ever owned. It was ever so slightly too big, but when he stood to have his picture taken in front of the photographer's backdrop, I confess to misty eyes and a lump in my throat. There were lots of young people leaving us that night with remarkable results, born of long hours of hard work, but few would have known just how hard it can be to walk into a room full of people, and believe yourself to be the least of them. Jack knew it daily, and that is why his turned out to be the greatest achievement of all.

Making connections

There are a number of lists in the New Testament which read like the one in 2 Peter. The passage is a route which begins with something broken and leads to something made whole or restored. The equation reads like this: support your faith with goodness, plus knowledge, plus self-control, plus endurance, plus godliness, plus mutual affection and finally love. Such lists can seem overwhelming or otherworldly until you see them working in action.

Beware of quick fixes. It is the slow impact of a good role model, consistent, patient and resourceful that is wisdom at work here. Genuine growth cannot be hurried and is not without setbacks. The final fruit of it is love, the cost of it endurance. The apprentice grows up while the master grows wrinkles.

This process can be best understood, not as that of a professor who informs, but of a master who reveals. Discipleship is best understood as an apprenticeship. The master shows, the disciple copies. It is the practice which changes the disciple. Failure is part of it, not to be avoided but to be embraced.

Teaching is a noble profession. I have been a teacher all my life and loved it. Mostly I have taught pupils. Occasionally I have taught apprentices. What is the difference? I think of David, who came up to me at the end of a lesson about career choices and said, "I want to do what you do." He didn't mean teach, he meant something else. He saw something he wanted in what I did. He had become my apprentice.

The finest example of apprenticeship I ever saw was Andy, who would give Jack a task, let him try, show him his mistake, and give it to him again to have another go. Until finally, when the time came, he could let him go for good.

Conversation starters

- Do you allow failure to defeat you or do you learn from it?
- What have you learned from watching people you admire?

Chapter 18

Foolishness

Someone in the crowd said to him, "Teacher, tell my brother to divide the family inheritance with me." But he said to him, "Friend, who set me to be a judge or arbitrator over you?" And he said to them, "Take care! Be on your guard against all kinds of greed; for one's life does not consist in the abundance of possessions." Then he told them a parable: "The land of a rich man produced abundantly. And he thought to himself, 'What should I do, for I have no place to store my crops?' Then he said, 'I will do this: I will pull down my barns and build larger ones, and there I will store all my grain and my goods. And I will say to my soul, Soul, you have ample goods laid up for many years; relax, eat, drink, be merry.' But God said to him, 'You fool! This very night your life is being demanded of you. And the things you have prepared, whose will they be?' So it is with those who store up treasures for themselves but are not rich toward God."

Luke 12:13-21

The long summer evenings were coming to an end. The days of tilting my motorbike around the Derbyshire peaks and troughs were over. Motorbikes are fun on a summer's afternoon, but on long cold nights the prospect of frostbitten fingers and black ice make the four-wheel variety of transport much more appealing. The attraction of two wheels was diminishing every time I had to put on layer upon layer of insulation. For some reason I never went in search of Harley-Davidson leathers. The bright yellow waterproofs I borrowed from school didn't make me look like a tough biker; I looked more like a large banana on a motorbike. Arriving at school in such a ridiculous outfit was not good for my credibility with the young people I taught. Scouring local papers, second-hand dealerships and trader magazines I was looking for a more comfortable all-weather alternative with a little more street credibility. It was time to buy a car.

The newspaper advertisement described a blue Ford Fiesta, a three-door hatchback with a 1.1-litre engine. It was four years old with one previous owner and a price of £500. At the time it felt like a great deal of money but the car would offer freedom, comfort and would save me from looking like a banana on a bike. When I arrived at the owner's house the car was parked outside and ready for inspection. It was navy blue with a sporty stripe down the side. The car was of its time, a bit more boxy than subsequent models, in which the square radiator grill and headlights would be replaced by round spotlights. The interior was quite basic and the seats were plastic; they were extremely hot and sticky in hot weather. It was in the last generation of those built of metal, chrome and dappled rust. Yet there was something about this car I really liked. Something intangible.

My initial reaction to the car did not change. I wanted it. Taking it for a test drive, I enjoyed the thought of driving it. The truth is, while the car struck the right cord, I had no genuine idea about the condition of it, whether it offered value for money or was a potential money pit ready to fall to pieces. I knew I'd enjoy driving it but I had little idea what its true condition was. I had never spent this much money on one item. It seemed like the best course of action was to call my dad, a practical man with years of car ownership experience. He would be a worthy adviser.

He seemed to spend so much time under the bonnet of his own cars and always took an interest in other people's.

My dad was some distance away so his advice would have to be over the phone. After a brief conversation about the car he said, "David, I'm going to ask you a few questions." I prepared myself, trying to recall all the owner had told me.

"Is there a service history?" he asked.

"Yes, definitely," I said.

"Have you started the car?" he continued. I had.

"Did the engine bite or splutter at all?" I told him that the rhythm of the engine was good.

"Have you looked underneath the car? Was there any oil or water on the drive?"

The answer to each of his questions was positive. He asked me more questions about the mileage, the wear and tear, and if there were indications of any neglect. We seemed to work our way through a long list as he searched for the sort of evidence that would give him a verdict.

Finally, after some time and as if to interrupt himself, he asked me a very different question, one which seemed to relegate all the others.

"David," he said, "do you love the car?"

It seemed incongruous, given the previous questions. After scrutinising the oil level, engine rhythm, and the state of the upholstery, this different focus caused me to falter. Thinking carefully about his question I replied as if I was about to get engaged to a Ford Fiesta, "Dad, I do!"

"Buy the car," he said instantly. "You have your answer."

I agreed. He had managed to confirm my intuition. I'd find the money and take the car.

It was some weeks later before I finally got to introduce him to the car. While out for a drive, hoping to impress upon him that we had made a good purchase, I asked him about his questions.

"What made you so sure the car was okay?" I asked.

He offered me a wonderful reply. "It's certainly not perfect," he said. "There is the first signs of rust in the bodywork and it has done a lot of miles." But then he added, "Once you have done a few basic checks, the question is not so much about what you are buying so much as your relationship to it."

"David," he continued, "the car will break down and when it does it won't feel expensive."

There is wisdom here. When there is no relationship with the item the most minor fault in a purchase will feel expensive. If I didn't care for the car, the cost of repairing something as minor as a failed headlight would hit hard. "Do you love the car?" sounds absurd, lacking in any considered reason, yet the real truth is that something can only be worth what it means to us. We forget this at our peril.

The principle applies equally to less expensive items. I recall Matthew as a little boy buying Alison a bar of chocolate for Christmas, his first genuine gift to her. I was quite sure that nothing I or anyone else could give her would mean as much. The look on his face when she unwrapped it was evidence enough that this small perishable item was worth far more than its monetary value.

There are lots of examples of missing this crucial point. Sometimes we go in search of bargains which turn out to be no saving at all because we didn't really want the gain we achieved. Getting two of something for the price of one is not a bargain if you didn't really need one in the first place, yet I have met lots of sensible and intelligent people who have been seduced not by the product but by the enticing offer. So often we allow the monetary value of something to determine our relationship with it. It seems that money can make a fool of us.

♟ Making connections

In Luke's Gospel, the famous story of gathering ever more grain into barns is not a warning against becoming rich. Jesus did not despise the rich. The story is warning against foolishness. In the story God calls the rich man a fool. At the time the story was first told, "fool" was a strong and uncompromising word. It is hard for us today to hear the severity of the phrase. It would have had the impact of a swear word. In Western culture a fool is often portrayed as something mild, a comic or a clown. Shakespeare made his court jester Feste a "fool that the Lady Olivia's father took much delight in" (*Twelfth Night*, 2.4). Feste was both witty and wise, the only character who truly understood what was happening. As a theatrical trick Shakespeare disguises his hero as a fool.

In the story from Luke's Gospel the opposite is true. It begins with the heir to a fortune arguing over his inheritance. The money isn't worth the division between the brothers. Jesus is responding by offering them a salutary lesson. The fool is the only person who can't see what is happening, he is consumed by a desire which blinds him to what he truly possesses. In Jesus' story, the rich man is a fool because he loses sight of the true value of things. Here a fool is someone who doesn't know what he has got until it is taken from him. In this story, the desire to protect oneself from the possibility of hardship leads the rich man to replace his faith in God with faith in his profits. Here is a disturbing paradox – when you think you are safe, you are in the most danger.

It may be possible to devote our lives to a false notion of the value of things. We can do it with an individual purchase like a car, but we can also do it with how we devote our lives, our energy, our priorities. The mileage might be a good question to start with, but in the end what matters is whether love features in what we give ourselves to. My dad's question was a good one. The car broke down frequently, but it never felt expensive!

Our relationship with money remains one of the most perplexing problems of our times. It is hard to understand how money influences us; whether we control it, or it controls us. The precise value of money is beyond anyone's control. It is as if money has a power of its own. As I write this piece, newsflashes on the internet are informing me of a stampede in Shanghai where at least thirty-six people, mainly women, have been killed and another forty-seven injured in a surge of people pushed one on top of another during a new year celebration. It seems likely that the stampede was caused by someone throwing what looked like dollar bills out of a third-storey window into the crowd. The people would not have intended such a catastrophe, but like so many instances of greed, somewhere someone else suffers as a consequence of our pushing for more.

Conversation starters

- Do you prefer to save money or spend it?
- Is there any risk in having more than you need?

Chapter 19

The road not taken

When many of his disciples heard it, they said, "This teaching is difficult; who can accept it?" But Jesus, being aware that his disciples were complaining about it, said to them, "Does this offend you? Then what if you were to see the Son of Man ascending to where he was before? It is the spirit that gives life; the flesh is useless. The words that I have spoken to you are spirit and life. But among you there are some who do not believe." For Jesus knew from the first who were the ones that did not believe, and who was the one that would betray him. And he said, "For this reason I have told you that no one can come to me unless it is granted by the Father." Because of this many of his disciples turned back and no longer went about with him. So Jesus asked the twelve, "Do you also wish to go away?" Simon Peter answered him, "Lord, to whom can we go? You have the words of eternal life. We have come to believe and know that you are the Holy One of God." Jesus answered them, "Did I not choose you, the twelve? Yet one of you is a devil." He was speaking of Judas son of Simon Iscariot, for he, though one of the twelve, was going to betray him.

John 6:60-71

Occasionally life throws a dilemma at us. Dreary-eyed, with half a slice of toast in hand, I pick up the mail. The letter on the doormat is about to dramatically disturb my peace and routine but I don't know it yet. It sits between a few bills and some junk mail. The unfamiliar handwriting on the envelope arouses more curiosity than the typeset on the other letters and so I open it first. It is a simple letter informing me of a vacancy. It is encouraging me to apply and asks me to get in touch if I am interested. It doesn't flatter to deceive; it is carefully written to suggest that someone somewhere thinks that I might be worth an interview. The words draw a smile since it is affirming to be thought of favourably, but I go off to work largely unaffected. It is just a kind letter.

It didn't turn out to be just a letter at all. Over the weeks that followed the words in the letter wouldn't leave me. They lingered in the gap between things, interrupting other thoughts without summons. The person who had written it had put an idea into my head. It is strange how such a simple suggestion can eat away from the inside causing so much disruption. My imagination conjured up images of leaving my present job for a new adventure and a fresh challenge.

I had thoughts about moving house, leaving all that was familiar. This prompted yet further images of saying goodbye to the people we loved and the safety of established relationships. The prospect of it all sent a shiver through my bones. Life was good. We didn't need a new adventure, so I contented myself with a more immediate distraction. "There is no question of leaving such a good life behind," I reassured myself, but the letter sitting next to the bread bin continued looking at me. As I lay in bed I could hear the letter downstairs, laughing away to itself.

Each time something difficult happened at work we found solace in the thought of moving on. Each time something good happened at work we found solace in the thought of staying. Without ever deciding as such, the letter had become the lens through which we were looking at the future. Should I apply or should I throw the letter away? Should we stay or should we go?

It was clear that just as in Robert Frost's poem "The Road Not Taken", ahead of us was emerging a fork in the road, a choice of journeys; one more familiar, one less travelled. We could stay with the route we felt we knew, or dare venture into the unknown. We had not invited the choice, yet it was now disturbing the peace.

One of the great skills in life is the ability to make good decisions. I have made many, but I'm hardly consistent, and my best decisions were more about grace than good judgement. Here we were, restless, wanting to fall one way then the other. We needed help, so we looked to others for advice as to how they made good decisions.

"Pray," said those with faith. "Pray and listen." Despite a faith in a God who listens, I have little experience of hearing a God who speaks, especially when it comes to responding specifically to my concerns and petitions. My experience is that generally God isn't very audible. There are Christians who will tell you that God told them what to do in this or that circumstance, but it often turns out that with a little more investigation their decision came from a "gut feeling", intuition perhaps, or desire. Most religious people don't tend to hear a heavenly dispatch in the form of a platform announcement in a railway station. We prayed, we listened, we heard nothing at all, except a lingering silence.

God's lack of audibility was something I had previously exploited in order to make a point. When I first became Head of Upper School, a job which meant leading a lot of school services – what used to be known as "assemblies" – I was conscious of how the young people were asked to begin each morning with a prayer. The idea that they were actually being listened to barely featured. The leader would begin, "We'll start our morning with a short prayer," and in response heads would drop as if they were puppets and someone had cut their head string. You'd see the young people looking in their bags on the floor to check they had brought their chemistry text book. It wasn't a culture of prayer so much as compliance with a reverential posture.

Wanting to challenge the routine, I concealed the deputy head behind the stage curtain one morning, a man with a powerful voice. As the young people filed in and sat down, I began, "Let us start the day with the prayer that Jesus taught his disciples..." Heads dropped and we began in four hundred monotone voices to recite the Lord's Prayer which begins, "Our Father, who art in heaven...", at which point the booming voice from behind the curtain rang out, "Yes... What is it?" Heads shot up. I then began a scripted conversation in which I would learn from God that he is interested in the ordinary detail of my life and wants to guide me through its difficulties. I was teaching them to expect an answer.

Ten years later I'm trying to make sense of a major dilemma I'm facing, longing for God to reply "Yes... What is it?" When I most needed a response, as C.S. Lewis describes, it was as if a door had been slammed in my face. God's reply to my confusion was silence. Was the message of my school assembly wrong?

The next advice we received was to seek the wisdom of others. We went to people whose judgement we respected. Almost everyone we asked appeared to offer contradictory advice. This only served to add to the perplexity. "Talk to those who will be most affected by the decision", we were advised, so we talked to our children, parents, our closest friends, our bosses at work. In these conversations it became clear that the people who cared about us didn't want the responsibility of influencing us. They would say such things as, "You must do what is right for you and your family." The problem was that we didn't know what was right for us and our family. We were going round in circles.

Books on effective decision-making advocate such strategies as writing a list of the positive and negative aspects of each choice. We sat down together with a bottle of wine to help us, and listed why we'd go and why we'd stay. It came to thirty-six in all. The list of positives and negatives seemed to cancel each other out. Advice gurus in articles also suggested making the decision, living with it, and seeing how you feel after a couple of days. This too we did. When we decided to stay we lamented the passing of an adventure. When we decided to go we grieved the life we were leaving behind. We were feeling tortured, trying to work it all out.

"Why don't you apply and let fate determine your destiny?" came some final friendly advice. This we did. Perhaps the only remaining approach was to trust the interview panel and surrender control of the situation to them. If the panel of inquisitors decided I was not suitable, it would take away our terrible restlessness and give us back our peace. If they chose me, we would walk out of our lives as we knew them, and venture onto the road less travelled. At interview I sat before a panel still a man divided and uncertain, quietly pleading with God to give these people the gift of wise discernment. They gave me the job. It was decided. We would let go of our established lives and move on.

We emptied our home, packed our belongings into a van, and dropped our keys through our own front door ready for the new occupants. It had been a threshold to a happy home. We drove silently away, wondering if we had done the right thing but not daring to ask each other. It was too late for all that. In the midst of all that unknowing, God remained consistently aloof. At that time, if some religious person had told me that we hadn't been listening to God properly, I'd have needed someone to restrain me. My faith in God hadn't been shaken, but the silence had been hard to understand, the consequences hard to live with. Sometimes trying to do what God wants isn't enjoyable and satisfying, it's tough and lonely.

Making connections

Over the years I had picked up the idea from religious people that God has a plan for our lives. The plan also came with a condition. If we listened and didn't stray from the path God offers, we would lead fulfilled and happy lives. The idea is attractive because it gives dignity and purpose to everything. As we pray, the mundane and difficult times acquire a capacity to awaken and transform us. The theology gives meaning to everything, because there is a big story going on – what James Hanvey SJ calls a meta-narrative. It is important to believe that God wants us to be available, ready and useable, that our lives are not vain.

At some stage though, we come across a challenge. What happens when we face two options, both morally good, at a time when God seems absent or deaf to our appeals? Do we rack ourselves with guilt for not listening properly, or blame an apparently indifferent God? I have met people who have headed in both of these directions. Some believe that God is ignoring their crisis, others blame themselves for being incapable of hearing God's direction.

Our dilemma about the job was far from unique. The lack of Godly lightning is well documented. In his meditations, Blessed John Henry Newman wrote: "He may make me feel desolate, make my spirits sink, hide my future from me. Still, He knows what He is about."

John Wesley, in his Covenant Prayer appeared to welcome such remoteness, "Let me be full, let me be empty, let me have all things, let me have nothing."

Great spiritual writers like Thomas Merton wrote of having no idea which way they were going. It seems that in a lifetime of faith there is a necessary emptiness at times, of not knowing rather than knowing, of confusion rather than clarity.

In John's Gospel we meet disappointment among the followers of Jesus. Some of those who admire Jesus are now finding the challenge of walking with him too much. There is the possibility of failure. They are not heading in the direction they had hoped. As Jesus approaches his destiny without an army, there is growing uncertainty among the followers and some start to fall away. Peter is different. Although there is a hint of reluctance in his tone, he knows he can go nowhere else. His relationship with Jesus has touched him deeply enough to know there will be no substitutes. No alternatives. No other prophet will do. He knows the Lord. Where do you go when you have come face-to-face with truth and the truth loves you? The only thing he can do is go where he doesn't know, or even where he would rather not.

During our painful time of discernment I realised slowly that we were not going to get an answer, a divine signpost from God. Not because God didn't have an answer, but because it was time to grow up. It was time to move on from worshipping a God who grants wishes. North or south, promotion or redundancy, marriage or friendship, stay or go, sometimes God wants us to learn to trust. This doesn't come from getting an answer. It comes from not getting an answer. Sometimes this can best be learned when the answer to prayer is an unrelenting silence. In my anguish over which way to go, God whispered in the wind, "I don't mind." Then added, "Do you mind if I come too?"

Conversation starters

- Do you involve God in decision-making? Does it work?
- What happens when you don't get an answer?

Chapter 20

Losing my nerve

So have no fear of them; for nothing is covered up that will not be uncovered, and nothing secret that will not become known. What I say to you in the dark, tell in the light; and what you hear whispered, proclaim from the housetops. Do not fear those who kill the body but cannot kill the soul; rather fear him who can destroy both soul and body in hell. Are not two sparrows sold for a penny? Yet not one of them will fall to the ground unperceived by your Father. And even the hairs of your head are all counted. So do not be afraid; you are of more value than many sparrows. Everyone therefore who acknowledges me before others, I also will acknowledge before my Father in heaven; but whoever denies me before others, I also will deny before my Father in heaven.

Matthew 10:26-33

It was a Thursday night after rugby training when the contest first came. I'd been expecting it for a long time.

"Dad," said Matt, "they've asked me to play on Sunday."

He was beginning to be recognised as a strong contender for inside-centre. Getting into the rugby team had long been his ambition and, with a lot of hard tackles and fitness training, he'd made it. As a family we had for some time been going to Mass on a Sunday morning at our local church and the opportunity to play for the rugby team clashed. The Sunday morning Mass catered for us because it included a special service adapted for children, particularly Matt's younger sister. It was a family service aimed at people like us. Now Matt would have to choose between the sanctuary and the sports field.

Herein lies a dilemma. There are two immediate responses. The first was to do the speech about what truly matters in life, how God holds us together, and how the other things we hope for will come our way in time. The problem was that through this reasoning countless young people encounter a spoilsport God who resides in the serious sanctuaries of wiser, more mature and sometimes duller adults, many of whom don't have the same sort of opportunities or conflicts of interest.

Matt was happier in the field, amid dirty boots, tested courage and strong friendships. Insisting that he come to church would turn God into an ogre who was ruining the good things in life and denying him the opportunities he was striving for. Do that to him for too long and he would start to resent the very thing we were hoping he would seek out and appreciate for himself.

The second response was to grant him his request. "Go on son," we could say. "Get on with your life, keep searching and know that the church is always here with an open door and a welcome home when you need it."

The problem with this was that God becomes little more than a genie in a bottle, someone to call upon when it gets rough, while the rest of the time being relegated to some third division of our priorities, remembered at Christmas and weddings with a nostalgic glance to appease and keep him on-side. Both responses are problematic. What is the right thing to do?

"Matt," I said, "on this occasion you are lucky to be a Catholic, because in our tradition we have what is called a Saturday Vigil Mass."

Matt knew what this meant. It meant, "Please come with us on a Saturday evening, and me or your mum will go with you on a Sunday morning. How is that?"

It all felt like a reasonable response. We were accommodating his wishes alongside ours. God could remain a priority without spoiling his sporting ambitions. After all, most adults arrange their religious observances to suit their timetables.

This compromise presented us with a new challenge. Back then (and it is different these days) the Saturday evening vigil was a rather sombre affair. The people who gathered were good people, of course, and kind, but they were for a large part elderly, especially to Matt, who stood out as one of the few young people there. Although many of them appreciated the presence of young people, it was for the most part on their terms. We were once informed by a fellow parishioner that this was "a quiet Mass", and as such should remain that way. Even the priest's attempts to enliven it were not always appreciated.

It is important to understand the liturgy as a solemn occasion, but when solemnity is in tension with a sense of celebration, it is often the young who walk away disillusioned. For Matthew at least, it seemed to him to be an hour of people much older than him mumbling.

"I'm not losing my faith," he once told me. "I just don't get what they are doing at church."

The sense of community we promised him in our parish was something he was truly experiencing in the rugby club, where he felt much more part of things. Despite this, he was happy to trade Saturday night for Sunday morning. He saw the value of both, and we were confident that we were not coercing or arm-twisting.

One Saturday afternoon, when Matt had been watching the seniors' game, I pulled up outside the rugby club. Winding the car window down I whistled at Matt and gestured that it was time we were heading off to Mass. It was a big thing he was doing for us, cheerfully leaving his social life to join us at church. I felt for him. No one else in his team followed such a routine.

As he walked towards the car he turned to a group of team mates and declared quite openly, "Lads, I'll see you later tonight, I'm off to church."

He slung his kit in the boot. Despite my conviction that this was a good thing to do, I winced. Winced because I know most people are not so naturally honest and open about going to church. These days you can be quickly stereotyped and so most people keep their religious convictions to themselves. Instead of the ridicule I expected from the lads, one of the lads shouted back, "Matt, can I come?" I laughed, assuming that he was joking.

"Yes," said Matt. "Get in," and the burly young lad ran towards the car.

"Oh no," I muttered to myself, thinking of the somewhat grey experience that lay ahead. Then another lad joined us. I had a car full.

As we drove towards the church I was looking at these popular young rugby lads in my rear view mirror.

"Dave," said Matt's friend, "I haven't been to church before."

"Oh no," I thought again. "Please let there be something about this situation that impresses them."

Matt was happily chatting away, and there I was, gripping the steering wheel with unusual stress. What will they make of the collective mumbling, the altar-server swinging the incense, the sitting, the standing, the genuflecting, the hymns old and even older?

As we arrived some were pleased to see the boys, some barely noticed them. As events unfolded before them they diligently did everything we did. They copied our gestures and read the prayers. I had to admire their efforts to fit in. On the way home they were kind enough to tell me it was interesting and later that night they were all out together again, back in their own world with their own age group.

There was something about all this that troubled me. The experience reminded me of the days I used to invite a girlfriend to family parties. There was inevitably a drunk uncle lying face down in a flower bed, my aunties arguing over their right to wash the pots, someone putting a lampshade on their head as a joke, a baby passed around like a prize.

The backdrop to this was the evidence of a Catholic upbringing. A plastic statue of Mary the Mother of Jesus with a screw-on crown, full of holy water from Lourdes. My mum's picture of the Sacred Heart of Jesus on one wall and my dad's picture of a Lancaster bomber on another. Taking a girl to my home made me vulnerable. This was my family, my mad family, and it said a lot about me that wasn't within my power to control. It dawned on me back then that, while I loved them, I was also embarrassed by them. The two seemed to go hand in hand.

Back at Mass with these boys the experience was similar. This is my church. There are warm, friendly people here. There are broken people here. Odd people. Some confused people. A few very timid people. There are statues of the torture of Jesus on the walls and incense coming out of what looks like a metal handbag, we are singing hymns a hundred years old, and using words like "Holy Ghost", and "consubstantial". For all its strangeness to the untrained eye, these people are here, looking to God to help them make sense of their lives, and there is something about them that I love. It began to occur to me that my embarrassment did not come from a bad place inside me, it came from caring about what people would think of it all. Introducing people to it is costly. It makes us look at it through unfamiliar eyes. Next time you take someone new to church don't be too surprised if it is you who change, not them.

👥 Making connections

Here I was, encouraging my son to recognise the value in coming to church. Yet it was his natural and unassuming effort to bring strangers to our service which caused me embarrassment. Irony of ironies. Who was doing the greater deed here? His inclination to share his parish with his friends revealed something of my hypocrisy. When was the last time I risked inviting newcomers to join us at Mass? When did I last risk embarrassment or rejection? He entrusted others to an event, while I winced at the thought of them joining us.

Jesus understood that it is one thing to be passively present, it is quite another thing to become an advocate of something. In the scripture Jesus is calling upon his followers to have courage, because it is only through bravery that others will come to know him. Matthew had a natural courage, unafraid that his rugby friends' experience of our musty gathering might lead them to ridicule or reject his church and him with it. How few of us who turn up week after week are brave enough to proclaim the very thing we find there, for fear that others might not see it? We wear it on the inside, since to bear it outwards would expose our embarrassment, as though someone were meeting our messed-up extended family.

Jesus makes a remarkable promise in this passage. Those who acknowledge him before others will be rewarded by having him speak in their defence. At his Confirmation celebration, a coming of age in the life of a fourteen-year-old Catholic, one pew was squeezed full of lads from the rugby club. Lads who turned up in suits and ties, showing respect for something they didn't understand. My heart went out to them. At the end of the service they had no idea what had just happened or why, but they shook Matt's hand and congratulated him. For all my religious inclinations and stipulations I had something to learn from this boy's courage before his peers and their respect for him. I'm sure that in the fullness of time, whatever he chooses to do on a Sunday morning, he is going to have a remarkable advocate at his side when he stands before the throne of God.

Conversation starters

- How do you feel about mixing different aspects of your life, work, friends, church and family?
- Which people make you reluctant to talk about faith and beliefs?

Chapter 21

Weak in the presence of beauty

Jesus went on with his disciples to the villages of Caesarea Philippi; and on the way he asked his disciples, "Who do people say that I am?" And they answered him, "John the Baptist; and others, Elijah; and still others, one of the prophets." He asked them, "But who do you say that I am?" Peter answered him, "You are the Messiah." And he sternly ordered them not to tell anyone about him.

Mark 8:27-30

O n the Bodrum peninsular nestled in a small bay is the little town of Akyarla. Back in the 1980s when we went there it was not established as a stylish resort. In those days Turkey was a largely undiscovered destination for Western tourists, just beginning to open up its coastline to its huge number of European neighbours.

The lack of amenities back then meant that it wasn't ready for the more sophisticated consumer. The minibus from the airport drove along the coast road until there was barely a road at all. When we got out, what we saw in Akyarla was simple and wonderfully unspoilt. The few beachside restaurants were family businesses, their staff keen to chat and practise their English once their shift ended. There were no companies pulling paragliders behind powerboats, no all-night clubs offering expensive cocktails to drunk teenagers. It attracted us because it was inexpensive but it was not refined. There were very few signs of how commercial such places would soon become, but back in August 1988 it was all still relatively innocent.

The arid mountains made a wonderful jagged backdrop. The sea was a rich azure. The pale sand burned your feet if you were foolish enough to step onto it. One beachside café played the Fleetwood Mac album *Rumours* over and over again because it turns out it was the only album they had. The days there lingered on for ever, the way they did when I was younger.

Around me were semi-naked bodies of every shape and size. Surprisingly, being surrounded by nakedness is not the delight some teenagers anticipate. Nakedness in the public domain and out of any context of intimacy is remarkably unflattering and quickly unimpressive. A serious-looking man strutting in a thong is at best comical and at worst horribly repulsive. In this situation, my sunny little world was about to be shattered by, of all things, yet another naked lady.

Amid the usual laughter on the beach I hear my name called by an incredulous female voice, "David? It's you," as if doubting her eyes. I stand looking for the source of this voice and there she is – Vicky, a work colleague from England.

"What is the chance of this happening?" she says in disbelief.

I work in an industrial town, an old-fashioned mining town, a place where it rains a lot, where people work hard, where Thursday is market day, and on Saturday people watch the football, and most of all, a town where people wear clothes when they are outside, all the time.

The initial surprise is followed by the surreal reality that this woman is almost totally naked but for a tiny thong. She is not naked in the way everyone else is on this beach, she is naked in a forbidden, this-isn't-allowed-because-I-work-with-you way.

Back at work, an accidental stumble into the ladies' changing rooms would cause this same woman to scream. Here, though, she stands before me with tremendous confidence, unfazed by her state. "I will not look down," I think to myself, "I will not stare." I'm confused at my own prudishness. I'm confused that the rules have changed. Why is something so seemingly wrong in one place, so suddenly acceptable in another? She is beautiful, confident and pleased to see me. Why then am I embarrassed, behaving like a boy avoiding looking at the top-shelf magazines?

As a child I received a healthy approach to family life, except that like most of their generation my parents struggled to communicate meaningfully what they had learned about sexuality. Unlike many men, my dad had the courage to speak to me about sex, but I remember wanting the "talk" to be over as quickly as possible. More informally, there was nothing more tangible than the tension arising from an impending sex scene on the television. Sex scenes did not present us with an opportunity to talk. My mum would censor it, probably from her own embarrassment. It unintentionally gave us the impression that bodies are shameful. The channels would be changed and we were all probably glad that any potential embarrassment was over. Dad could re-emerge from behind his newspaper.

Here in Turkey I was behaving like my parents, wanting the nakedness to go away. It is a strange thing to want to hide from beauty. Here was a blonde young woman, standing unashamed on a beach, and I was longing to find her a fig leaf. She was acting like Eve before she ate from the tree of knowledge and I was acting like Adam after it. It is not difficult in these circumstances to be in awe of beauty and at the same time behave as though something isn't beautiful at all. It is not difficult to feel weak in the presence of beauty, to run away from it, to sense its power and want to supress it. Cultures have struggled with this confusion for centuries. There are few desires as powerful as our physical attraction, and yet our efforts to control it can cause us to act hypocritically or to hide from each other. If we are not careful we can become crude and permissive on the one hand or prudish and repressive on the other. What was I to do, talk about the weather or compliment her tan? Vicky was happily unconscious of her appearance. Her beauty, like the beauty of many young people, is perhaps one of the most powerful forces on our planet. Which is why it may cause so many different reactions.

As a teacher I would accompany young people to their school-leavers' prom night. As they arrived in their dresses and dinner jackets it was easy to be literally stunned by their beauty and somewhat in awe of it. Girls, at times so anxious and unconfident about how they looked, had no idea how completely perfect they were in their black dresses. It was always a privilege to see the young men or women emerge from behind the teenage angst and acne. They were so beautiful that at times it moved me deeply to see them like this, daringly entering into the brave new world that lay ahead of them. Whatever we have to say about young people, good or ill, they have the advantage of beauty. That is their gift.

At first, like Aphrodite, beauty is most obvious in the soft seductive surface. It is skin deep. Later, beauty takes on many other guises. One morning I was driving around a suburb of Cardiff. During a torrential rainstorm I was straining to locate the whereabouts of a school. To cope with the sheer volume of rain my windscreen wipers were working at their fastest pace. As I slowed down to try and locate exactly where I was, I found myself on a very steep hill, a short distance from another primary school. I parked the car in order to put the destination address in my satnav. As I did so, two young women walked past me on the pavement beside my car. They were having to lean forwards against the incline, pushing heavy prams up the steep hill. Their heads were right down, facing the pavement. They were pushing their babies home, having dropped their older children off at the school gate. These young women were soaked to their core by the downpour and they looked terribly cold. The rain was dripping off their noses. I could almost hear God saying to me, "Aren't they wonderfully and perfectly made?"

Here was another form of beauty. I was momentarily distracted by them. Looking at them I knew they were only a few years away from the dance floors. Only a short time before they were falling stupidly in love, racing off to the toilets in nightclubs together to refresh their mascara. Here they were, so soon after, giving their lives to their children. No makeup on their faces, just rainwater. Their beauty was in their strength, dedication and selflessness. There are few things more stunning and yet so ordinary than the love a mother can feel for her children. This was generous beauty, on a wet Monday morning in a damp windy suburb.

As I have got older I recognise beauty more readily, although it still presents itself in the most unexpected places. As a little boy I was told not to stare at people. Sitting in church I couldn't help but stare at the people going to communion. Fat people, thin people, old people, young people making their way to receive communion. It was only their appearance that struck me. Nice coat, old coat, funny hat, beard.

"Don't stare," mum would say, especially if I caught the eye of a friend and they'd pull a face. It was one of these occasions when I recently caught myself looking at a man making his way to the altar to receive communion. Every step looked painful, a concerted effort. Pushing his stick forward so that he could lean on it, with each step he would make little progress and a queue built up behind him. He was, though, beautifully determined, resolute, his gaze fixed on the prize. He was running his race to the end. Behind him, his daughter, a woman in her fifties, ready to catch him, but skilful enough to hold back, knowing this was something he had to do himself. Behind her a woman from the Philippines recently arrived in the parish, carrying a child on her hip. Behind her an ex-Marine, recently retired, trying to make sense of his new life out of the navy. Behind him a woman we knew whose marriage was broken and was rebuilding her life without him.

It was then, that I thought I could hear the words again, "Aren't they beautiful?"

"Yes, Lord," I said in answer, "they really are." And for just the briefest of moments I could see it. Rather than look away with embarrassment , I had a tear in my eye.

Making connections

Tradition suggests that we can understand something of God from his creatures' perfections. Anything that is true, good or beautiful indicates the transcendence of God. Truth and goodness are often referred to in religious terms, but beauty poses a few more problems. One of these is that recognising beauty leads us to want to possess or control it. This can becomes a lust or obsession and we can begin to covet, hide or disguise it, become jealous of it, or lose our confidence in its passing. We can also deride its absence, diminishing what we see as ugly or useless.

In the multi-layered story of Adam and Eve there is a wonderful insight into the same struggle. God is happy to show them the tree of knowledge which bears the fruit of knowledge, but asks them not to possess it for themselves. For our happiness, God's gifts have to be received rather than taken. In this way we can appreciate our lives in a different way. After taking fruit from the tree Adam and Eve's eyes are opened and they can no longer look at each other for the confusion of shame and desire they feel. In a loving touch, God then makes clothes for his creation, even though they have disobeyed him.

Beauty is a gift. In whatever form it takes – physical, intellectual, aesthetic, moral or spiritual – our disposition is to treat it with respect and gratitude. The physical beauty of the young is a gift and we should not deny, denigrate or seek to own it. It is why we can be moved at the mere sight of a young woman in a wedding dress. God chose to give beauty to young people and it should be honoured, not least because in time it will be taken from them. This is not an accident of nature. God wants to teach us something important about the world.

Beauty has many guises. In the scripture passage Jesus is asking what people see when they look at him. Some might see a carpenter's son, a local upstart. Those who listen might hear a rabbi whose wisdom is beyond his years. Those who ponder his teaching might perceive a prophet. Peter, whose gift it is to see beyond all this, recognises truth, goodness and beauty. As a consequence, he is able to see the Messiah.

In the same way, we learn through the events of life to look beyond what we first see. With patience and the wisdom of years comes new insight. In time our eyes are opened to the way in which beauty, truth and goodness are entwined. We begin to perceive something spiritual in a woman pushing a pram or the determination of an old man with a stick. Before long beauty is everywhere, even in what was once deemed by us to be ugly or depraved. God's first gift is a simple beauty, but look long enough and you'll see it not just in the art galleries or the hilltop view, but in a person with the courage to do the right thing for the right reason.

Conversation starters

- What different kinds of beauty do you see?
- Has your appreciation of beauty changed?

Chapter 22

Unthinking

You are the salt of the earth; but if salt has lost its taste, how can its saltiness be restored? It is no longer good for anything, but is thrown out and trampled under foot. You are the light of the world. A city built on a hill cannot be hidden. No one after lighting a lamp puts it under the bushel basket, but on the lampstand, and it gives light to all in the house. In the same way, let your light shine before others, so that they may see your good works and give glory to your Father in heaven.

Matthew 5:13-16

There were two worlds I used to leap into from time to time in order to escape my own. The first was to travel and the second was cinema. It is not that I have had an unhappy life. I have been truly fortunate. Sometimes though, a brief escape can help you to look at reality differently, things you might otherwise overlook.

The Ritz Cinema was a regular feature in my youth. Like so many cinemas in the 1970s it was struggling to remain viable. It was first opened in May 1939 in an age before television arrived in people's homes. During the war its regular Pathé news bulletins would keep the town in touch with the outside world. This grand picture palace had enjoyed more prosperous times, but by the 1980s it was faded and smelled of sad decay. In its final days the lady in the ticket booth would provide you with a ticket, follow you up the stairs to the door of the auditorium, greet you again and punch your ticket with a hole-punch. Later she would sell you a tub of frozen ice cream or a drink of Kia-Ora in the interval. If you went often enough she'd know your name. The curtains would sway open and you'd be quickly engulfed in a thick blanket of smog. If the film was lousy you could be entertained simply by watching the projector send shafts of light through the moving cigarette smoke.

For my parents, whose courtship took place in the early 1950s, the Ritz provided a rare opportunity for a little privacy. The movies offered neutral territory, a darkened world to escape from the cold in a time when people couldn't afford their own place. With limited finances their honeymoon consisted of a trip to the cinema to watch *Weekend in Paris,* and my mum recalled how they had to sit separately on the bus on the way home because it was crowded. It was a different world. There would be revival just around the corner, but things were not going to turn around quick enough to save this lovely old building from demolition.

The interior had been an art deco masterpiece, with thick red carpets, hanging chandeliers and large mirrors. There was no hint of the multiplex supersize cinema chains, blockbusters with online booking, or melted cheese on nachos. It was in a timeless lovely old building like the Ritz that I had an encounter with unthinking me.

There was not much in the way of patience in my younger self. Years later, sitting alongside my girlfriend in another cinema, the film was working towards its grand finale. As the credits began to roll I had no particular desire to know who the dubbing mixer was or who co-ordinated the stunts. As name after name worked its way down the screen I was conscious of the queue of traffic which would shortly be leaving the car park.

"Come on," I said. "Let's get out of here."

We weaved our way along a line of seats occupied by people in less of a hurry.

"Sorry," I said, turning towards the lady whose handbag I had just kicked.

"Sorry," I said again, as people stood to let us past, their seats flipping up as they did so.

When I got to the end of the row I turned towards the screen, put my hand onto the end armrest and genuflected. Genuflection is a gesture of respect for a tabernacle in a Catholic church. Catholics briefly go down onto one knee before entering or leaving a pew as if to bow before what they regard as a sacred presence. Here was I genuflecting before Mel Gibson and Danny Glover in *Lethal Weapon*. I heard one or two people laughing, who were most likely Catholic. Other people thought I was either drunk or had dropped my wallet.

After getting over my minor embarrassment, what troubled me was not the fact that I did something in one arena which belonged in another, but that I was acting upon impulse, without any conscious thought. I discovered in a cinema that it is possible to put all sorts of things on autopilot, even the things I do in church. So much of my behaviour had become unthinking routine.

After I told this story at a conference, an elderly lady came up to me and said, "I did something weirder than that." When she had told me, I said, "Ivy, I'm going to tell everyone what you have told me, and I'm going to make you famous!"

One day while shopping in Derby, this sprightly eighty-something was pulling her two-wheeled shopping trolley onto the bus. Approaching the driver to pay her fare, she put her hand in the used ticket bin and, as if dipping it into a holy water stoop, proceeded to make the sign of the cross in front of him.

The very Catholic gesture of putting your right hand to your forehead, chest and shoulders, in the same way that some footballers do as they run onto the pitch, made the bus driver laugh out loud. Ivy and I had discovered that it is possible to get so lost in the routine and familiarity of doing things that we forget why we are doing them. Making these gestures in the wrong place at the wrong time was posing new questions for us.

Travel provided me with another means of escape. In our twenties Alison and I would head off with very little money, a couple of rucksacks, and a four-hundred-page international railway timetable. One of the joys of Western Europe is that it has a high density of cultures and histories squeezed into a comparatively small corner of a continent which also boasts long beaches, snow-peaked mountains and vast expanses of lowland woods and lakes. Connecting it all is one of the oldest and remarkably criss-crossed rail networks in the world.

Three weeks into a rail trip across Europe and you are not quite sure which statue of which king you are looking at, and in which city. They all look the same. A big horse, a colonel's arm raised, sword at the ready, covered in disrespectful pigeons. Where are we again? It could have been near the Frauenkirche in Munich, or was it St Stephen's Cathedral in Vienna? The remarkable tiled zigzag roof on one building, the legend of the devil's footprint in another. Who cares? We used to call it "culture fatigue". It is possible to sit in Hohenzollern Castle or Neuschwanstein Castle and not really care, even though you have seen them in movies like *Chitty Chitty Bang Bang* and have long anticipated visiting them. Despite the remarkable scene that surrounds you, the preoccupation is what time the youth hostel opens or whether there is a grocery shop nearby. It can all too quickly become a thoughtless routine. As for tomorrow – another day, another statue.

It was in a car driving home from a cinema that I first properly asked the question, "What is it that I bow to in my life? What do I really truly regard as worthy of my genuine submission?" Some of the people around me at the time would have said "Nothing – bow to no one," but isn't that rather sad? Do I really want to be the greatest thing in my universe? In my very effort to escape reality in the cinema and on my travels, I'd learnt something about it. The risk of losing a sense of occasion is a dangerous feature of our lives. What starts off as amazing and incredible can become automated. We don't necessarily stop what we are doing, rather we carry on doing it unconsciously. Going through the motions without a conscious decision. If we saw a miracle happen every week, would we stop seeing them as miracles?

Making connections

Salt can do three things. Firstly, it preserves. It stops perishable food from becoming putrid. Secondly, it gives added flavour. Thirdly, salt purifies because it burns germs and impurities. The phrase "Rubbing salt into my wounds" originates from the experience of hearing a painful truth. In these three ways, being salt was a powerful performance indicator for Jesus' followers. For the good of others as well as themselves, the disciples were to be spice in a world where lives can decay and lose their flavour.

The teaching here is not simply about losing faith or settling for mediocre. There is more to this. When salt loses its taste it doesn't stop being salt. The salt continues being salt, but it becomes ineffective. We can carry on unaware that we have lost our saltiness. A few years ago I was invited by a religious order to explore with them the vision and "salt" of their foundress. They humbly and respectfully recognised that after a hundred and fifty years of dedication and service they were losing sight of their original spice. What had once stirred their hearts and made them attractive to others had become diluted. They still existed and functioned, doing good work, but they had lost their sense of daring and adventure. They found themselves busy looking after old buildings and older members and had become swamped by administration. It can happen to any of us. They hadn't lost their vocation or their busyness, but they had lost their salt.

At the time of Jesus, tasteless salt would eventually have to be discarded, having outlived its purpose. Useless, it could be burned off or cast onto the land; as the scripture says, "Thrown out and trampled under foot."

In Leonardo Da Vinci's famous fifteenth-century portrayal of the Last Supper, Judas is there of course, still being a disciple among disciples. He is portrayed clutching a small purse possibly containing silver coins, a symbol of his compromise and betrayal. He is unaware that his elbow is knocking over the salt cellar. There he sits at the table, listening to Jesus with the others, but he is losing his taste right before our eyes. He knocks over and loses the spice of his convictions: his betrayal is foretold.

The secret is not to hide, disguise or bury our convictions, hence the association in the scripture of salt and light. Judas is carrying the burden of an inner spirit at odds with his outer behaviour. The metaphor of salt is quickly followed by one about light, to shine before others. The beauty of wearing a conviction on the outside is that it remains vital, tested and raw. The alternative is to find yourself going through the motions, genuflecting in cinemas.

Conversation starters

- When do you act without thinking?
- How might revealing your convictions help to restore the daring and adventure in your life?

Chapter 23

Friday night and Sunday morning

The woman said to him, "Sir, I see that you are a prophet. Our ancestors worshipped on this mountain, but you say that the place where people must worship is in Jerusalem." Jesus said to her, "Woman, believe me, the hour is coming when you will worship the Father neither on this mountain nor in Jerusalem. You worship what you do not know; we worship what we know, for salvation is from the Jews. But the hour is coming, and is now here, when the true worshippers will worship the Father in spirit and truth, for the Father seeks such as these to worship him. God is spirit, and those who worship him must worship in spirit and truth."

John 4:19-24

As an adviser to teachers I often found myself at the back of large halls watching various assemblies and acts of worship. The idea was that the pupils would gather around some moral or spiritual focus at the beginning of the day. Often the course of events went something like this: entering the stage from both sides, a gang of about six boys aged ten wearing their school ties around their heads would be making lots of noise and hurling abuse at the group opposite. The inevitable fight would break out centre stage in which all the lads would throw pretend punches and roll about on top of each other with flailing fists while the entire school would look on. The teacher whose class was performing would stand at the back of the hall, wishing she had supervised things more closely from the beginning and prevented things from escalating.

Reluctantly, a boy would emerge from the back of the stage. It was he who had the pivotal responsibility of playing Jesus. I always felt sorry for the boy who was given the role of Jesus. Usually, it was a role no one wanted, so it usually fell to the pupil least able to protest. As the boy proceeded, the mass of legs and arms would disentangle and a small corridor would open up in the pile of fighting bodies. Jesus, now centre stage, would proclaim in a stilted voice: "Boys, boys stop that at once!"

The boys, now standing in two groups, would listen obediently to Jesus, who would continue: "You have heard it said, an eye for an eye and a tooth for a tooth... but I say... " – he would briefly glance down at the small card in his hand which contained his misspelt prompts – "... love your enemies," he would continue, "and... pray for those who prosecute you." The class teacher would roll her eyes in embarrassment.

The two gangs of boys would stand to attention and, as if instantly converted by his words, one would reply, "You're right, Jesus!"

Now reconciled, the gangs would step forward to shake hands. A piano would start the tune of a familiar hymn, and a few forthright adults would start the singing. The power of this moment was striking. The audience had once again been treated to the unintentional and yet strangely common message that the world was much more fun before Jesus stepped in and put a stop to it all. Why is it that, in our effort to communicate a life-giving message, we so often end up doing the exact opposite? Can it be that our efforts to enjoy ourselves can seem at odds with what we hold as right and just?

The Victorians built beautiful, grandiose buildings. Their sewage works incorporated stained glass, town halls were topped by magnificent domed roofs and train stations had the impressive appearance of stately homes. Manchester Town Hall is one such place. As I stood in the main hall to address a large conference of young people I was very conscious of the huge portraits on the walls. Many were of the city fathers, a variety of nineteenth-century philanthropists and entrepreneurs whose ingenuity and business sense had led to an industrial revolution which swept the world. They all gazed upon me from inside these great dark murals. The men in the paintings had founded a great city between them, and this building was the culmination of their work and ingenuity. What would they make of this young pretender standing in this town hall, whose legacy could not hope to match their own?

The theme of our day together was "Spirit and Truth". Since the Nicene Creed describes the Spirit as the giver of life, I began by asking these young people when they felt "truly alive". These eighteen- and nineteen-year-olds had little difficulty approaching the question: "When I have a good laugh with my mates," answered one young man. That wonderful feeling, we all concurred, when it hurts to laugh because your lungs won't inhale for the laughter. Another student spoke of adrenalin-inducing moments such as extreme sports and rollercoasters. Others spoke of sexual chemistry and the thrill of falling in love. They reminded me of the excitement that comes with a returned glance on a dance floor. They spoke of moments of achievement such as passing a driving test or collecting exam results. These young people were full of life, theirs was a world of music, dance and daring. Feeling alive was associated with moments of discovering what could be achieved in a world of immense social and intellectual challenge.

After a lively discussion I asked the same group about their understanding of truth and where they look for it. This second question threw them into a more reflective mood.

"Is truth about evidence?" asked one student.

"Truth is about making decisions," said another, raising the question whether there is pre-ordained truth and how we might recognise it.

A further conversation ensued about whether something is always true, or whether it depends on other factors. What became clear was that the young people were searching; some were praying, many were asking deep questions about God's existence. They were trying to navigate their way through the noise of their lives. Many agreed that the discernment of truth requires silence away from stress and anxiety. Their search reflected internal turmoil about who they are and who they are destined to become.

These two questions expose a problem. On the one hand there is Friday night, a place of life and spirit. Here the music is fast and vibrant, the night-time full of anticipation. There is beer, laughter, noise, friendship, and energy. In this space people are having fun. On the other hand there is Sunday morning, when a mood change is needed. The music here is reflective and slow. There is strong coffee. Things become clearer in the morning. Perhaps it is time to think things through, to reflect, to pray, to go to church. This is time to contemplate and to face up to life's challenges.

What happens if our Friday nights and our Sunday mornings become divorced from each other, as if we become a different person in each? What happens if I choose one rather than both? The danger is that without Sunday morning, Friday night becomes superficial, trite, and if I spend too long there it becomes a lonely place. On the other hand without Friday night, Sunday morning can become sullen and intense. Without Sunday morning, Friday night can become sarcasm without humour, sex without love, wine without joy. Without Friday night, Sunday morning can become self-righteous without mercy, ritual without conviction, prudishness without passion. The risk is that if we trade-off spirit against truth, our Fridays become empty and our Sundays become dull. Sunday-focused people can end up over-exaggerating the importance of the tiniest detail, while Friday-focused people can devote their lives to running away from the bigger responsibilities.

The skill of course, is to bring our experience of Friday night and Sunday morning to bear upon one another. To ensure our experience of Friday isn't so shallow that we never fully take to the water, while at the same time not drowning in the depths of Sunday morning. Because if we are too earnest and otherworldly we lose our capacity to welcome people off the dance floor.

Making connections

To take any passage in Jesus' encounter with the Samaritan woman away from the rest is to lose something from the narrative. Here though, along with several other occasions in John's Gospel, it is worth noting the reference to worshipping in "Spirit and Truth". The woman is posing a question about who is right – are the Jews who remained in exile right, or are the Jews in Jerusalem right? Jesus is not interested in the geography or politics of her question. What matters is her openness to worship in spirit and truth, through joy and reason, with energy and wisdom. Jesus is truth, and the Spirit will guide her to him. After the encounter she is so full of Spirit that she returns to her village to announce the truth to everyone. She is effervescent and sure.

Once on a parish retreat I found myself enjoying an evening meal with a group of young people and two lovely religious sisters, both in their seventies. I encouraged the young people to ask the sisters about their lives. One of the girls asked, "Do you ever jump up and down on the beds in the convent?" The sisters were wise but unusually on this occasion they missed the question. The question was a good one. The young people knew that these nuns were unlikely to bounce up and down on beds, but the question wasn't about jumping, it was about joy. One of the sisters replied, "No we don't jump on the beds, the sisters are quite old." "Oh," replied the teenager, and the questions dried up. It is hard, especially for young people, if there is a gap between Friday and Sunday, no matter how narrow the gap. Perhaps this is why Pope Francis is calling upon Christian churches to rediscover the virtue of joy.

The Victorians built everything as though God is present, churches and workplaces. Perhaps if we could find the connection between Friday night and Sunday morning our lives would be more joyful too.

Conversation starters

- How connected are your Friday night and Sunday morning?
- Do you suffer from becoming either too serious or too trivial?

Chapter 24

The grateful disciple

Above all, clothe yourselves with love, which binds everything together in perfect harmony. And let the peace of Christ rule in your hearts, to which indeed you were called in the one body. And be thankful. Let the word of Christ dwell in you richly; teach and admonish one another in all wisdom; and with gratitude in your hearts sing psalms, hymns, and spiritual songs to God. And whatever you do, in word or deed, do everything in the name of the Lord Jesus, giving thanks to God the Father through him.

Colossians 3:14-17

We don't choose our neighbours. Statistics appear to indicate that as many as one in ten of us will move house at least in part because of the difficulties we experience with our neighbours. More worryingly, almost one in three of us will have a dispute with our neighbours at some stage in our lives. The most common causes of tension include late-night noise, boundary disputes, untidiness, car parking and more rarely, aggressive behaviour.

Of course, sometimes our neighbours can be saviours. I think of my nephew, who at the age of three climbed out of his ground-floor bedroom window very early one morning and headed out on his tiny tricycle in his dinosaur pyjamas. Back then he didn't have a great yearning for freedom or ambitions of making his own way in life. Arriving at the house next door he knocked on the front porch to ask the elderly couple who lived there for a biscuit. Realising what had happened they lovingly brought him back to my brother. Nowadays he has to live with that story at every family gathering.

We have lived next to all sorts of people and by and large we have been very fortunate. Sometimes, especially when the children were little, it may have been us who were the neighbours you'd want to move away from.

I can think of two contrasting experiences of neighbours, from my childhood. Firstly, Dorothy comes to mind. She was often in her pristine garden. When we were little she would have to dodge footballs, frisbees, tennis balls and all manner of flying debris from our games. Her sunny afternoon peace and quiet would be interrupted by noisy contests and occasional squabbling. Regularly she'd appear at the fence, her spindly fingers appearing over the lattice panel fence. She'd quickly be surrounded by us as she passed over chocolate bars and treats of all kinds. Occasionally she'd give us pocket money to spend in the shop.

As we grew up, Dorothy would remind us how much she enjoyed hearing us play in the garden. She'd tell us how laughter was infectious and would make her smile. With a hint of loneliness she would explain how her son was returning from Australia next summer and how she couldn't wait to see her grandchildren and how quickly they were growing up. She would tell stories of her daughter's recent move to Birmingham and how she would be going to stay with her soon. In the retelling of her stories it was clear that her scattered family meant everything to her. She lived for the next opportunity to catch up with her grandchildren whose images adorned every available wall and shelf space in her house. We seemed to remind her of her own grandchildren.

Then there was Ken. I recall as children we were reluctant to knock on his door. He too loved his garden. There was a greenhouse stocked with bedding plants, borders neatly weeded and a pretty rose garden. Whenever our ball went over his fence there was a dispute as to who would fetch it. To recover it meant enduring his wrath. Even as children we knew that he was not a bad man, just unhappy, and that made him difficult to approach. Sometimes he was not angry with us, but his anger was enough to make us want to forget the ball altogether and go and do something else.

What was it about these two neighbours that made them so different? On reflection what we knew about them did not explain their different reactions to our noisy chaos. Both had known times of austerity and plenty. They had both been married, happily it seemed. They had both raised families and their children had children of their own. They had both suffered the loss of a partner and learned to live with grief. So why did one person see a ball in their garden as a blessing and the other as a curse? Why did one rejoice in the disruption and the other bemoan it? The answer, I have come to believe, is gratitude.

St Paul regularly encouraged the early Christian communities to continually give thanks. Why should we always give thanks when often we feel like Ken and not Dorothy? Gratitude, it seems, is sometimes a powerful feeling – but most of the time it is a decision.

As I drove home from work one night I was repeating over in my head a conversation with a colleague which had annoyed me. The injustice of the situation was causing me frustration and anxiety. As I replayed the meeting in my mind I found myself getting angrier still. As I pulled up in our front yard, I took the keys out of the ignition. Next to it I had stuck onto the dashboard the word "gratitude". It was there to remind me. Seeing the word didn't make everything alright. When I looked at it I didn't hear happy music. Squirrels and rabbits didn't jump onto my bonnet and start cleaning it with their tails. Gratitude is not a warm cheesy moment made up of primary colours and candy.

The word reminded me that I was not ready to get out of the car. It reminded me that on the other side of the front door of my house was a five-year-old girl who would run to greet me when I walked through it. It reminded me that I shouldn't go in with a face that could burst balloons and sour cream. So I sat there for a few minutes breathing deeply, in and out. As I got out of the car I gathered myself enough to remember to bend down and greet her like we had been apart for far too long. Before I knew it, puberty would catch up with her and turn her into an anxious and self-conscious teenager. So I knew to be grateful for her embrace while it lasted. Once I had reminded myself of this, I was ready to go in.

As I walked through the door, sure enough she ran and threw her arms around me. I picked her up and threw her into the air. I was still preoccupied with being a strong and worthy, dedicated and considerate father. But it was her arms around my waist that did the healing. In the face of love's embrace the pain of the day can lose its sting.

Like so many times before, I thought, "You stupid man David Wells." There I was imagining that I was doing Emily a favour. A disposition of gratitude simply helped me to receive. If I could hold onto a little of it, this child's love would dissolve the stresses of the day. Amid tension and tiredness gratitude heals.

Ken was not a bad man. God loves him as dearly as he loves Dorothy. The difference between them is that despite the sorrows of life, Dorothy had stayed grateful, and so she found it easier to count the blessings rather than the cost.

Making connections

My eldest son fell in love with a girl in a village a few miles out of town. He was too young to drive. It was perhaps only a twenty-minute drive, but it meant frequent favours picking him up and dropping him off. Many evenings were spent pulling up outside his girlfriend's house to bring him home. On the drive back one night we had a usual chat about nothing in particular and as we pulled up at our home he said, "Thanks, Dad."

"No problem," I said, getting out of the car.

"No," he said, calling me to attention. "I mean thank you," and he looked at me.

The thank you wasn't coming from a casual place. It was coming from somewhere deeper. "Behold the man," I thought, as I realised his thank you was not an expression of politeness as it had seemed before. This was gratitude. They are different. For Meister Eckhart this is God's most desired prayer, a thank you which comes from deep within us. Parents recognise it too and when they hear it, they are almost caught off guard.

For St Ignatius the most abominable sin is not greed or anger as many would imagine today, but ingratitude – for, as he explains, "It is a forgetting of the gracious benefits and blessings received." For Ignatius, God is generous and to overlook this is the beginning of all corruption. To practise gratitude is to keep in mind that everything is gift. When we look to all we have as a gift from God it prevents us from taking it as our own by merit. If we believe we have an automatic right to what we have, we lose the joy of receiving it. We become consumerist, inclined to complaining and then slowly become dissatisfied when life doesn't quite fulfil us. As long as the food on my table remains God's gift to me, I can delight in it. When I lose sight of that, something of the joy of it can be lost and I'll start focusing on its deficiencies. If I'm not careful, in a world where so many are hungry, I'll be complaining that the service is too slow.

People who exercise gratitude can begin to see a blessing in all things. There are times when joy is lost and the weight of the world sits heavily on our shoulders. In these times we have to dig deep in order to find the blessing. I always liked the role of Reb Tevye, the father in Fiddler on the Roof, who greeted each challenge as yet "another blessing". Jewish wisdom decrees that if you look hard enough you'll find a blessing in everything. Even in the Monday mornings. Some people learn this lesson early and it stops them becoming the sort of miserable neighbour who resents the appearance of a football over the fence.

Occasionally a thank you comes from a deep place within us. Sometimes I look to the skies and cry the words almost helplessly. Sometimes, and briefly, God's goodness is overwhelming. When those moments come there is an opportunity to please God in the same way that gratitude can please us. Try it. It stops you becoming a grumpy old fool.

Conversation starters

- For what are you truly grateful?
- Have you caught yourself suffering from ingratitude?

Chapter 25

The woman in the grey coat

But Mary stood weeping outside the tomb. As she wept, she bent over to look into the tomb; and she saw two angels in white, sitting where the body of Jesus had been lying, one at the head and the other at the feet. They said to her, "Woman, why are you weeping?" She said to them, "They have taken away my Lord, and I do not know where they have laid him." When she had said this, she turned around and saw Jesus standing there, but she did not know that it was Jesus. Jesus said to her, "Woman, why are you weeping? For whom are you looking?" Supposing him to be the gardener, she said to him, "Sir, if you have carried him away, tell me where you have laid him, and I will take him away." Jesus said to her, "Mary!" She turned and said to him in Hebrew, "Rabbouni!" (which means Teacher). Jesus said to her, "Do not hold on to me, because I have not yet ascended to the Father. But go to my brothers and say to them, 'I am ascending to my Father and your Father, to my God and your God.'" Mary Magdalene went and announced to the disciples, "I have seen the Lord"; and she told them that he had said these things to her.

John 20:11-18

One of the most difficult jobs known to humanity has to be that of the long-suffering supply teacher. Such staff are employed on a temporary basis to enter into the classroom in order to cover for the absence of the regular teacher.

The task is difficult for one simple reason. Names. The knowledge of a student's name indicates a relationship. Without that knowledge the teacher is vulnerable.

On many occasions as a senior teacher I would be called to calm a disruptive class only to arrive and meet a supply teacher on the verge of a breakdown. Almost invariably a story would be told in which the pupils were being disruptive, the teacher would ask someone's name, the name of a fictitious or absent pupil would be given, and so it begins. Everyone knew, except the supply teacher. Without a name, the teacher had no recourse to action. There could be no sanctions without names.

As a young teacher I learned a simple trick. Having been warned about a particularly challenging class of fourteen-year-olds I was keen to establish my authority. When you meet a class for the first time it is essential to get off on the right footing. Almost everything is decided in the first ten minutes. As they sat at their desks I knew that more than anything what I most needed was their names. Choosing to say a little about myself, I walked between the desks, explaining how much I disliked fourteen-year-olds and how horrible I could be. It was my instinct to start eccentric and relax later. As I walked between them giving my introductory speech, I noticed that many of them had put their exercise books on their desks. Glancing from behind their shoulders I made a point of looking carefully at the names on their books.

As I arrived back at the front of the room I turned to them and said, "Okay that is enough about me, now it is your turn."

I looked towards the students who names I had seen and began, "Callum, tell me something about you."

Startled, he immediately replied, "How do you know who I am?"

"Callum," I said ominously, "I know everything about you, what you had for breakfast, what football team you support. What you think about me?"

"How?" he said. "How do you know these things?"

"It is my job to know," I said, and, turning towards another row of desks, continued, "Helen, how about you? Tell me something I don't know about you."

By now I had unsettled them. They were getting the idea. Once I had their names I had authority, but much more importantly, I had a relationship. Without names I was alienated.

Similarly, as adults we know that we do not belong until we are known. It is one thing to greet a person with "Welcome", but the word is transformed when we add a name. Greeting can be institutionalised, assigned to a rota of volunteers. Church communities are very good at greeting people at the door, but welcoming is a commitment to some kind of relationship – and it is the use of someone's name which elevates a greeting to a welcome.

My own skill of welcoming has a lot to be desired. My capacity to remember names is woeful. I can ask for a name and lose it within seconds. Once I have asked a person's name I am reluctant to ask a second time. Quite often at Mass I would notice a beautiful elderly lady in front of me. Despite the onset of various ailments including arthritis, she was never sullen or ill-tempered and her smile could light up her face. She always clasped my hands warmly and asked how my children were doing at school. She would remind me that she has prayed for them. She would follow the Mass in her prayer book with her failing eyes pressed close to the page. She was spritely and cheerful despite her suffering. When she died, the parish secretary kindly put a photograph of her at the back of the church with an invitation to pray for her and her family. Seeing her name I realised with regret that I had never learned her name, remembered it, or used it when I spoke to her. Lazily, she had become known to me as the woman in the grey coat. It was a poor way to extend a welcome. How could I be a neighbour to her without a name?

After that I resolved to ask people their names more often, and dare to ask them again no matter how stupid I looked.

Making connections

We see people not merely by sight. As we get to know each other we see much more than their outward appearance. At first glance we are strangers to each other – a physiology, striking in one way or another, but no more than that. In this beautiful passage from John's Gospel Mary sees a gardener. A messenger perhaps. She sees only someone who can give her information. She is distracted by her state of grief, distressed by the scandal of a dead body that has been taken. She is not looking for anything more than information. She is looking for a body and can see nothing else.

In order to help her look beyond her distress, Jesus uses her name. It is a moment of profound connection. In using her name she is jolted, propelled into a revelation of who she is talking to. In this moment a relationship is instantly re-established. As with the woman at the well, Jesus has seen beyond her state and into her heart. Now, Jesus invites Mary to do the same. She replies by calling him "Teacher". The title is not the reference to a profession but to a relationship. When Mary uses the word "Teacher", she is speaking from her experience of the Lord. It is her description of what he did for her, rather than a job title. She is honouring him. This remarkable incident is a defining moment in the Christian story and is intensely personal. Through the intimacy that comes with the use of a name, we encounter the resurrection of Jesus. From that moment Mary's life, and the life of the followers of Jesus, will never be the same.

Disciples are not volunteers. Disciples are called by name. In a pastoral letter from the US Bishops, they describe the Christian calling thus: "He [Jesus] does not summon disciples as a faceless crowd but as unique individuals." Ultimately the Christian yearns for this calling by name, which brings with it an encounter, a personal relationship. When our name is called in this way, we are changed.

Sitting in a tutorial one day, hoping that my university tutor would not realise how little I knew, I found myself giving a badly researched paper on some aspect of English local history. As the session came to an end and my fellow students left the room, my professor asked me to stay behind. I expected him to mercilessly dismantle the assumptions I had made in my paper, which he was inclined to do from time to time.

Looking over his spectacles he said, "David," as if what he had to say had some significance, "you should think about teaching."

"Thank you," I replied somewhat taken by surprise by an unusually personal comment, "I will give it some thought."

His use of my name and this simple and brief conversation changed the course of my life. It was a calling. I'm not sure if he knew it, but I did.

Conversation starters

- What does your name mean to you?
- How do you feel when someone uses your name?

Chapter 26

What the dog left behind

They came to Bethsaida. Some people brought a blind man to him and begged him to touch him. He took the blind man by the hand and led him out of the village; and when he had put saliva on his eyes and laid his hands on him, he asked him, "Can you see anything?" And the man looked up and said, "I can see people, but they look like trees, walking." Then Jesus laid his hands on his eyes again; and he looked intently and his sight was restored, and he saw everything clearly. Then he sent him away to his home, saying, "Do not even go into the village." Jesus went on with his disciples to the villages of Caesarea Philippi; and on the way he asked his disciples, "Who do people say that I am?" And they answered him, "John the Baptist; and others, Elijah; and still others, one of the prophets." He asked them, "But who do you say that I am?" Peter answered him, "You are the Messiah." And he sternly ordered them not to tell anyone about him.

Mark 8:22-30

Good artists have a knack of revealing much more than the subject of their painting. John Everett Millais was a remarkable artist. By the time he was eleven he was the youngest student ever to be admitted to the Royal Academy. Like many artists his work was not without critics or controversy. His painting "Christ in the House of His Parents", painted in 1850, caused consternation because it positioned Jesus in what was considered an undignified and unsuitable home and portrayed him with ginger hair. Charles Dickens loathed the painting and described the portrayal of the Jesus' mother Mary as, "So hideous in her ugliness that she would stand out in the lowest gin shop of England." The scene generated such discussion that Queen Victoria requested it be brought to the palace so she could see for herself what all the fuss was about.

It is a later painting by Millais, "The Boyhood of Raleigh", in 1870, which has had the greater impact upon me. I really appreciate Millais' portrayal of the young Walter Raleigh with his friend, captivated by the storytelling of an exotic seafarer. Millais used his own sons as models for the painting.

It should be a compulsory part of every teacher's training to visit Tate Britain on Millbank and look at what is happening in this painting. The most moving and poignant aspect of any teaching is when a teacher captures their students to such an extent that they forget themselves. The expression on the boys' faces is what teaching is about. One can only imagine the words of the storyteller and the tales he is telling. Millais knows that the young boys will someday go in search of what they are hearing. If ever a painting caught a sense of wonder in the face of a child, this is it. The other reason I enjoy looking at the painting is that it was painted in Budleigh Salterton, just a short distance from where I live. The wall which provides a small part of the backdrop for the painting still stands.

Sometimes we find ourselves in what could be a real-life painting. I'm standing on a footbridge at Matlock Bath in Derbyshire's Peak District. It's a beautiful summer day. Below us the River Derwent cascades through a gorge. In front of us two limestone cliffs rise abruptly out of the bushes on the riverbanks. Topped by emerald green shrubs, these wonderful cliffs stand tall and defiant. The large sheer blocks of limestone are interrupted by impertinent small trees growing precariously out of fissures in the rock. Crows circle above us. The river continues relentlessly downwards. The waters ripple, crystal clear, as clean as drinking water. In the wide, shallow, stream-water we see trout, roach and grayling swimming furiously against the flow of the river, merely to remain stationary.

Sam has pulled himself out of his buggy and is standing next to me. He holds onto the railings with one hand, his ice cream in the other. He pushes his face against the gaps between the bars, straining to see the fish. He points to one and then to another, his big eyes surveying the scene. He makes me smile. Having this little boy has taught me to see the world differently, the way I once did. A tractor, a fire engine, a donkey, a rainbow, a man with a very large nose, these things have become things to mention once again. I'm surprised that I am enjoying explaining the simplest of things. In my complexity I had stopped seeing them. Stopped caring about them. Now though, this boy was teaching me to kick piles of leaves, pick up worms and point to the colour red. I realise that my life had changed for the better. There is something satisfying about losing the complexity and sophistication of life for the sake of watching the bin men coming to empty all the bins. Because of Sam, we know the bin men's names.

Seeing the beauty of the carved landscape, the endeavour of a climber making his daring way up the rock face, the fish whose colours blend with the riverbed, I put my arm around Sam's shoulder and looking through the railings with him I say, "Isn't it beautiful?"

"Dad," he says, as if it is his turn to point something out. "Look," and pointing downwards with the littlest of fingers, he shows me what he has found by the side of his shoe – the biggest dog poo he's ever seen.

He can't take his eyes off it, and then finally looking at me wide-eyed he says, "It must have been a big dog!"

Once again he's taken me by surprise. He isn't ready for limestone cliffs and emerald shrubs – for him, the dog poo will do.

Back in the Tate Gallery something else is happening. While looking at Millais' painting from a few metres back, a couple stand in front of me. They want to know what the painting is and who painted it. They stand right next to it, too close to truly see it. They look for a small label below the picture. They then look in their guidebook and glance upwards. Neither the title of the painting nor the image itself arrests them. It is not a painting they recognise and they move swiftly on.

An artist friend told me amusing stories of people who work their way around an entire gallery looking at the labels rather than the paintings. It is the easiest thing to miss the picture for the tiny plaque that describes it. It is easy to forget to stand back. As small children we were able to see what is beneath or next to our feet, but only those who learn to look further beyond get the adventure they are looking for.

Making connections

We are born into a world where detail delights us. We could be lost in wonder and awe at the sight of a raindrop as it serpentines its way down a pane of glass. My efforts to introduce Sam to the bigger picture taught me to enter into his world. The danger comes not from observing what the dog left behind, but from struggling to see beyond it.

In a conference in Guadalajara in 1996, Cardinal Joseph Ratzinger warned that when faith wears down it "degenerates into small-mindedness". This shrinkage transforms Christians into, "Mummies in a museum", added Pope Francis. When we stop pointing to the horizon, to the vastness of things, to mystery, we get caught up in all sorts of scrupulosity. The very desire for a bigger picture is what draws us to the seaside. There is something very revealing about being small creatures before a big canvas. Children see the wonder and vastness in small things. Adults need a bigger vision to maintain that wonder.

In this passage from Mark's Gospel, the healing of the blind man at Bethsaida describes sight being restored in stages. This is followed by the passage in which Jesus asks his followers who people see when they look at him. Some see only what is in front of them: a rabbi, a teacher or a prophet. Like the blind man, some see beyond what first appears, to the greater narrative, Jesus, the chosen one of God, the Word made flesh. The disciples are invited to see an eternal vision, a bigger picture. Jesus is imploring us not to stand so close to the canvas of our lives that we fail to see the picture we are in. When we trust that our lives exist inside a story bigger than ours, we do not exhaust ourselves with trying to control the smaller details. Like the sailor in Millais' painting, good religion will always point to the bigger-than-us.

When the detail becomes the source of our anxiety, it is the glance in the direction of the big picture which holds us together. It was once my place to visit a school after the sudden and unexpected death of a pupil. "It's amazing," said one of the staff, "the tragedy has pulled us together." In the aftermath of the things that really matter, the bigger things, we stop falling out over photocopying, car parking, budgets, and comments made in yesterday's meeting. In the absence of the bigger picture we'll fall out over whose chair we are sitting in, whose pew we are sitting in, and one day we too are fossilised. Take a look at Millais' painting, there is an adventure to be had, if only we could see beyond what is immediately in front of us.

Conversation starters

- Where do you go to get things in perspective?
- Does the detail of things ever distract you from the bigger picture?

Chapter 27

Stand by me

Meanwhile, standing near the cross of Jesus were his mother, and his mother's sister, Mary the wife of Clopas, and Mary Magdalene. When Jesus saw his mother and the disciple whom he loved standing beside her, he said to his mother, "Woman, here is your son." Then he said to the disciple, "Here is your mother." And from that hour the disciple took her into his own home. After this, when Jesus knew that all was now finished, he said (in order to fulfil the scripture), "I am thirsty." A jar full of sour wine was standing there. So they put a sponge full of the wine on a branch of hyssop and held it to his mouth. When Jesus had received the wine, he said, "It is finished." Then he bowed his head and gave up his spirit.

John 19:25-30

Schools are strange worlds. At one level there is a strong sense of formality. A bell indicates where you should be. Rules govern almost every movement, clothing, behaviour, chain of command. Schools are fenced in, secure and regulated environments. Underneath all the systems and policies, however, are a thousand young people caught up in the pressures of compliance and dissent. Some of them channel their energy into rebellion, while others become dangerously stressed over passing the test and meeting expectations. In an ordered world there can be lots of insecurity, extreme stress, anxiety, intimidation, and the relentless struggle to be popular. You have to be tough or toughen up quickly, because navigating your way through it can be profoundly challenging. We can forget that the playground can be as tough as the "real" world.

There is no doubt that school can be wonderfully absurd. I recall my much-maligned physics teacher trying to put a fire out in the waste-paper bin by stamping in it, only to find the bin stuck on the end of his foot. As he hopped around the room with his foot on fire trying to shake the bin free it was hard to come to his rescue with tears of laughter streaming down our faces. Such moments stand out far above any fear we had of the bigger kids, or the frustration at the sometimes mundane and boring days. We should be cautious about recalling school as "the best days of our lives". For Liam, it really wasn't that good.

Liam was one of those boys who was difficult to like. For that reason, we tried even harder with him. He was awkward around his own age group and preferred the company of adults. He spent a lot of time near the staff room door. His approaches to the staff lacked timing. He'd want attention at moments we could least offer it. He seemed to struggle to read people, their moods and expressions. He couldn't pick up nuance, hints or subtlety. These things aren't on a curriculum. You either pick them up or suffer confusion. Liam was suffering. He wasn't bullied so much as ignored or overlooked. He wasn't rude or malicious, just lacking awareness, and he quickly irritated people. All the rules and formality of schooling couldn't resolve this, because the rules he broke weren't in a manual anywhere.

After school one evening I have a pile of books to mark. The classroom is peaceful and empty. The silence of the corridors makes a change from the unbridled energy that flowed through them just minutes earlier. The late afternoon sunshine sends shafts of light onto the desks. I love this time of day – the calming atmosphere of a school which has breathed out its pupils and is inhaling a little evening serenity. There is the distant sound of a floor polisher and occasionally the sound of fellow colleagues in conversation as they head home. I'm working my way down a pile of books, all sadly predictable – the girl whose handwriting consists of large loops, another whose page is almost a work of pristine perfection without a blemish to be found, and a boy whose tight writing looks like it has been blown by the wind, all leaning drastically forwards. There is another whose writing is barely legible, and whose pen has leaked and smeared across the page heading.

As I pick up Liam's book a piece of paper falls to the floor. It is a note, in writing I don't recognise. I assume it is for me: "Liam couldn't do his homework this week because..."

But it isn't a note like that, and it isn't for me but it's too late – I've read it. It's a short note written by Liam's mum, that finishes with the words, "Liam, don't forget what I told you. Things will be okay. I love you. Mum."

It turned out the letter wasn't for Liam after all – its message was for me, even if it was unintended. The note was a stark reminder that I needed to look at this boy with the eyes of love. Our greatest teachers love us insofar as they want what is good for us. Not as measurements of their own performance, but out of sheer vicarious pleasure in our advancement. If I was to be of any service to this boy I had to look at him the way his mother did. I was ashamed that for all my teaching about love, I'd failed to love him properly.

All this reminded me of another mother. In the summer of 1998 Richard Bacon had the best job in the world. At least that is what most people thought. He worked as a children's TV presenter for the programme Blue Peter, a job that would take him all over the world. In October that year the *News of the World* reported that Richard had been taking drugs. He lost his job immediately. Richard has enjoyed a successful career since and regretfully has to recognise that he will probably be remembered as the presenter who was sacked from children's television.

This story though, isn't about that. Shortly after the event his mother was interviewed on the radio. As I was driving along I listened to the line of questioning. The interviewer was probing. As I recall, the conversation went something like: "You must be very disappointed, what did you say to him?" he asked. Her reply was powerful. She replied simply, "He is my son." There was a short but wonderful silence. She had spoken a truth. Our misdemeanours, no matter how great, will not blur the eyes of love. Anyone fortunate enough to be loved by a mother, will know that long after their friends and neighbours have deserted them, the love is undimmed in the eyes of the woman who bore them.

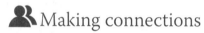Making connections

Mark, Matthew and Luke paint a similar picture of the moment Jesus dies. In each case the women who followed Jesus from Galilee are there, watching from a distance. Matthew and Luke both mention among others Mary Magdalene and Mary the mother of James and Joseph. While the disciples have scattered in fear of being arrested, the women are still there, watching, albeit from a distance. Mary Magdalene will be the first to meet the risen Jesus. The presence of these women at his death is important, since they will serve as witnesses to his resurrection. In John's Gospel Mary the mother of Jesus is standing at the foot of the cross. The geography is important to John. Mary is not observing, she is involved, participating in the scene.

In the scriptures, solidarity is understood by who you stand by. "If I do judge, my decisions are true, because I am not alone. I stand with the Father, who sent me," says Jesus (John 8:16, NIV). Similarly, Mary is in solidarity with her son. She accepts his fate as he does. She is not fighting against the will of her son who is giving up his life for ours. Her motherly love does not seek to prevent him from fulfilling the will of his Father or drinking of the cup that has been given to him.

Mary's position, standing as she does, is a sign of strength. In the scriptures, to stand is a sign of defiant strength: "No city or house divided against itself will stand" (Matthew 12:25). Mary is not beating the floor in distress like Rachel weeping for her children. She is not remonstrating with the centurion or screaming at the injustice of the torture. Here we see a woman who has entered into the deeper mystery of Jesus' death. She has pondered in her heart all that has been asked of her and in the moment of her greatest agony, we see her standing at the foot of the cross, an image of courage and understanding. She stands in defiance of the sin which has put her son on the cross. The sin of the world has not overcome her, neither does she succumb to it. She, like her son, is giving her life, not having it taken from her.

Love often begins with attraction. The romance which follows is to be enjoyed, but it is ultimately its own reward. When people truly love us, they go far beyond buying flowers. Love stands in solidarity and strength, defiant of all that condemns it. Love stands by us when we are vulnerable. Love stands by the unpopular person when they are ignored and overlooked. This is what Liam's mum showed me. I can lose sight of this greater love. When we stand by vulnerable and discarded people we are doing what Mary did and Jesus before her.

One very important measure of what makes us Christian, is who we stand by. What makes a school a truly Christian place is what happens to the most vulnerable child in it. What happens to Liam.

Conversation starters

- Who do you stand by, and who stands by you?
- Who would you stand by, whatever they did?

Chapter 28

Lifting our hands

*You must see what great love the Father has lavished on us
by letting us be called God's children – which is what we are!
The reason why the world does not acknowledge us is that it
did not acknowledge him. My dear friends, we are already
God's children, but what we shall be in the future has not
yet been revealed. We are well aware that when he appears
we shall be like him, because we shall see him as he really is.
Whoever treasures this hope of him purifies himself, to be as
pure as he is.*

1 John 3:1-3

T he 15th of June was one of the hottest days of 1996.
Roasting under an unrelenting sun I was squeezed into
Wembley Stadium along with seventy-six thousand other
football fans. The occasion was the European Championship and
we were watching England playing Scotland. Watching this
match was part of a stag weekend for a group of us from
Nottingham. Despite the enjoyment of a raucous weekend, the
match itself turned out to be extraordinary for another reason.

The first half of the game was a disappointment. Both sides
were anxious not to concede a goal and played cautiously,
cancelling each other out. There was no flair, no moment of
audacious skill, just anxious sport. As the second half began
there was no shortage of tension in the stadium. Both sets of fans
were restless. The game had brief moments to stand up for, the
crowd grew louder and finally the deadlock was broken with a

goal by Alan Shearer. The Scottish team remained resilient. It was becoming a better game, but not much better.

At the far end of the pitch, the furthest away from our viewpoint, England conceded a penalty. David Seaman saved the ball by diving in the right direction. The ball hit his elbow. It was a piece of cruel misfortune for Scotland. It looked as though the game would stumble its way towards an unmemorable 1-0 victory. Standing among my friends I was becoming slightly disappointed in the spectacle. More than a result, I was looking for a moment of genius to savour. Quietly and in the strange sort of privacy you can sometimes achieve in a big noisy crowd I said a discreet prayer: "Lord, you gave Paul Gascoigne an amazing gift, give us a glimpse of that gift today."

Moments later the ball was at Paul Gascoigne's feet. Receiving a pass, Gascoigne lofted the ball over the Scottish defender Colin Hendry and before it could return to the ground he ran past the player to volley it into the goal. It was a genuinely sublime piece of skill you couldn't coach into a player. To do that sort of thing you need to be able to imagine it, have the confidence to believe you could do it, and then the skill to deliver it. You either have that gift or you don't. The next day the newspapers called it an "I was there goal" – and I was. I was behind that very goal looking at an act of God-given talent. The collective cry of the England fans around me was deafening. We had been treated to a lifelong memory of the beautiful game.

There is an opinion which would suggest that God wouldn't answer this sort of prayer. I would caution against anyone thinking that God favours one team over another. There is also coincidence of course, and the probability that every so often such requests are going to be met with the desired outcome. The story is not about the credibility of the experience. Whatever the theological conundrum, I was momentarily stunned that I had seen what I asked for. As the crowd around me roared (and roar is no exaggeration) I looked to the sky and uttered a spontaneous "thank you", and I meant it. The demonstration of the player's genius felt as if a gift had been handed to us. We were jumping around, hugging each other, arms outstretched to the sky, singing, laughing and punching the air. As we turned back to the pitch to see our heroes, we were united in the belief that we had just witnessed something remarkable. We all had our arms raised to the sky as we sang. It was the most natural response of us. No one thought to ask if such behaviour was appropriate. It was natural.

Long before this event and as a young adult I found myself caught between two rather unfortunate alternatives. There was my local church, a respectable, prayerful and yet unfortunately languid experience. The people were loving and kind, but the expression of faith lacked any outward expression of joy. There were genuine attempts by some parishioners to inject some vitality, but others were reluctant to respond. Sometimes it felt like hard work for the priest, trying to muster a forthright response. The gathered assembly was sincere, but collectively lacked enthusiasm. The toned-down behaviour made me think that, while we said together words like, "We lift up our hearts to the Lord", most of the time you wouldn't have got that impression from our faces.

The alternative was something I found in the maritime city of Southampton. In the middle of a respectable suburb was a set of university halls of residence which became home to a Christian conference each summer. I'm not sure what got me there but I recall being rather resentful to be put in a "discussion" group, on a programme which looked to have little free time. As I perused the timetable for the days ahead I found myself irritated by it. Workshops entitled "Praise and Thanksgiving" didn't appeal to me. Given my desire for something more joyful, I was surprised at just how reluctant I was to thank God and be grateful. Amidst such enthusiasm, I wanted to go home.

To make things worse, everyone except my girlfriend and I seemed to have a look of anticipation. People greeted each other with warmth and were keen to talk to us. We didn't quite know where to place our personal discomfort except to moan to each other every time we were left alone. "Too much," I thought to myself. "This can't be real."

My problem, I realised, was that while I found the tiredness of some local parishes dispiriting, I had also been conditioned by it. I wanted the heat turning up, but only to my level of comfort, certainly not to the friendliness of these people. I'd become so used to having a private faith that their expressions of joy seemed to threaten my comfort. I contented myself with thoughts that all this joy wasn't genuine. I wanted a t-shirt which read "Keep Out" or "Go Away", accompanied by a picture of an Alsatian dog. Were they right to be enthusiastic or did I have a right to bark at them?

There were a few things which surprised me. Unlike my local parish there were many other young people here. Equally disconcerting was the music, enlivened by the idea that singing was a means to express gratitude. Although much of it wasn't known to me, it was easy to pick up and was sung with real gusto, just like my friends at Wembley. Most worryingly and I have to admit, somewhat embarrassingly, some people were lifting their arms as if reaching out to the God they were praising. This wasn't anything like Michelangelo's representation of an almost indifferent Adam on the Sistine Chapel. As St Augustine said, "He who sings prays twice." Through their gesture, they believed they were adding weight to the words they were singing.

This did not come naturally to me at all. Despite the fact that our priest used such gestures in our liturgy, the action of the congregation was generally to keep their arms down. It wouldn't be forbidden to raise them, but it would be seen as a bit weird. Some Catholics would open their hands in front of them at waist height during the recital of the Lord's Prayer, but that is about as far as most people would go. At this conference though, there were fewer inhibitions. Some sat, some knelt, some sang with their arms in the air. Why is it that a simple range of gestures so natural and acceptable in a football stadium could cause so much inner consternation in a place of prayer?

My disposition was to dismiss all this hand-waving, but something inside me was prompting me to learn from it. Had I become too proud, too serious, and too uptight? So tentatively, I opened my hands to see what it felt like.

Much later, when the children were little, each of them did something natural and impulsive. Tiny hands would raise up in my direction in total expectation. When they lifted their hands in the air they demanded a reaction, "Raise me up", their hands said, but without the words. What struck me was my impulsive response. It was impossible to resist. Had they used words, the request would have lost some of its potency. Expectantly raised arms communicated many things, dependency, the desire for encounter, complete trust.

"Should my faith not look a little more like that?" I thought. "If I am a child of the Father, is it so inappropriate a gesture?" I had never been completely comfortable with it until, taught by my children, I learned to raise my arms more freely. Out of the sight of many, sometimes with others, I would raise my arms in a simple gesture of acknowledgement and gratitude. I avoided situations in which such a gesture would be a distraction. Slowly though, in humility as much as enthusiasm, I learned to lift my hands to the Father, because I need him like my children need me. One of the easiest places I ever made this gesture was in 1996 at Wembley, in front of seventy thousand football fans. One of the hardest was at church.

Making connections

In Psalm 134 as an expression of gratitude, we are encouraged to lift up our hands in the sanctuary. This can be a bit risky in many churches. People who do so, suffer the label of being "happy clappy". The label carries an accusation of being oblivious to the suffering of others. Someone might also be accused of drawing attention to themselves. Slowly, out of sensitivity to each other, we have lost gestures of praise and thanksgiving. Strangely, the secular world can adopt these gestures more freely without the same anxiety. Delight and appreciation expressed enthusiastically are deemed appropriate for those we admire. It is ironic that we could cause more outrage raising our hands in a church than we would in a pub in front of the television when our team wins. If only we could thank God with the same enthusiasm we thank our heroes.

The issue, it seems to me, is whether we see ourselves as children of a loving Father. That is not to be childish, but to be dependent upon the one who raises us up. In John's letter, he writes "Beloved, we are God's children now." Sometimes to be a follower of Christ calls upon us to set our faces like flint, to be courageous, tough or solemn. On the other hand there are times when it might help to raise our hands a little, childlike, in humble recognition of our need, sometimes in praise, sometimes in silence. Jesus teaches us to call upon the love of his Father, Abba. Sometimes the most natural response is to do that with our hands. Perhaps that is a good place to finish this book, with a grateful heart expressed through an opened hand offered to a Father who loves us.

Take a look of the cover of the book. That is me. Because in the end, the most important prayer you'll ever say is "Thank you" – and although you don't always feel like it, God delights in our deeper thank you. Spoken or not.

Conversation starters

- How do you feel about people lifting their hands in prayer?
- Can you open your hand now, no matter how hard your life is, no matter how discreetly, even under the table in front of you, wherever you are, and find something inside yourself to thank God for?